Hathcock and Associates

1751 Welcome Rd

Williamston, SC 29697

Printed in the United States of America

Because of the dynamic nature of the Internet, any web address or links contained in this book may have changed

Biblical Symbolism

By David B Hathcock

Chapter one

We are going to be discussing objects and situations and symbolism used in the Bible, God's, word to try and get the true meaning of what our Heavenly Father wants us to learn or know in this time in history. But first, we should all have a complete understanding of the meaning of symbolism. As given in our modern dictionaries, I will show three definitions of the English word symbolism.

These definitions are:

(1) The use of symbols to represent ideas or qualities.

"He has always believed in the importance of symbolism in garden art."

(2) The symbolic meaning attributed to natural objects or facts.

"the old-fashioned symbolism of flowers."

(3) An artistic and poetic movement or style using symbolic images and indirect suggestion to express mystical ideas, emotions, and states of mind. It originated in late 19th century France and Belgium, with essential figures including Mallarme, Maeterlinck, Verlaine, Rimbaud, and Redon.

Your choice to accept or reject these definitions.

The following work is mine only with the help or guidance of the Holy Spirit, I believe. Again, you can learn from this work or reject it. My only desire is to help my fellow Christians. **We'll start in the book of Genesis.**

Genesis

- "In the beginning, God created Heaven and Earth."

My question is:

The beginning of What?

Perhaps, you think this phrase means the 'beginning of everything.

6

But is this true? Think now! I ask this because, in the book of St. John, it states, "In the beginning was the word," so which was the real "beginning?" Both verses are right; only one verse tells about the start of this Universe, and the other tells about the start of this physical world or 'age'; two different points of 'beginnings' or different ages starting. Most of the time when the bible uses the word 'world', a better translation from the ancient manuscripts would have been 'age' or time period.

The book of St John explains how everything was brought into existence.

(1) In the beginning, was the Word, and the Word was with God, and the Word was God.

(2) The same was at the beginning with God.

(3) All things were made by him, and without him was not made anything that was made.

(4) In him was life, and the life was the light of men.

(**5**) "And the light shineth in darkness; and the darkness comprehended it not.

(**6**) "There was a man sent from God, whose name *was* John.

(**7**) The same came for a witness, to bear witness of the Light, that all *men* through him might believe.

(8) He was not that Light but was sent to bear witness of that Light.

(**9**) *That* was the true Light, which lighteth every man that cometh into the world.

(10) He was in the world, and the world was made by him, and the world knew him not.

(**11**) He came unto his own, and his own received him not.

(**12**) But as many as received him, to them he gave power to become the sons of God, *even* to them that believe on his name:

(**13**) Which were born, not of blood, nor of the will of the flesh, nor of the will of man, but of God.

(14) And the word was made flesh and dwelt among us, (and we

<u>beheld his glory, the glory as of the</u> <u>only begotten of the Father,) full</u> <u>of</u> grace and beauty.

I placed this part of John's gospel so the reader can see and understand the Bible is addressing two different ages.

I know most of God's children don't understand the different Ages" of this world, so I'm going to try to explain the various "Ages," the best I can.

After the original creation, which was perfect, and was created by the Word (Jesus Christ) as stated above in the excerpt from the book of John; God created all his children, known as Angels, and all the different animals of which we still find bones and remains today. God created all things for his pleasure, as stated below.

Revelation 4:11

Thou art worthy, O Lord, to receive glory and honor and power: for thou hast created all things, and for thy pleasure, they are and were created.

But all things didn't stay that way. One of God's chosen archangels wasn't satisfied. This son of God was Lucifer, and he started a rebellion in God's own Kingdom. As we read in the book of Revelation, 12:1, and the rest of the verses:

(1) And there appeared a great wonder in Heaven; a woman clothed with

the sun, and the moon under her feet, and upon her head a crown of twelve stars:

(**2)** And she being with child cried, travailing in birth, and pained to be delivered.

(3) And there appeared another wonder in Heaven; and behold a great red dragon, having seven heads and ten horns, and seven crowns upon his heads.

(4) And his tail drew the third part of the stars of Heaven, and did cast them to the earth: and the dragon stood before the woman which was ready to be delivered, for to devour her child as soon as it was born.

(**5)** And she brought forth a man child, who was to rule all nations with a rod of iron: and her child was caught up unto God, and *to* his throne.

(**6**) And the woman fled into the wilderness, where she hath a place prepared of God, that they should feed her there a thousand two hundred threescore days.

(7) And there was war in Heaven: Michael and his angels fought against the dragon, and the dragon fought and his angels,

(8) And prevailed not; neither was their place found any more in Heaven.

(**9**) And the great dragon was cast out, that old serpent, called the Devil, and Satan, which deceiveth the whole world: he was cast out into the earth, and his angels were cast out with him.

This rebellion was the start of God's problem with his children that he created. Of course, if Lucifer had been the only Angel in the resistance, God could have banished him or killed him, but this was his child, and Lucifer wasn't alone in this rebellion. A third of God's children followed him in trying to take over God's throne.

In the biblical scripture given above:

It is my opinion; mine alone, you may have yours.

Woman------------Mother Israel

Sun -----------------------God

Moon ----------------------Satan

12 Stars -------- Jacob's 12 sons

Red Dragon ------------- Lucifer

Devil -------------------- Lucifer

Serpent -------------------Lucifer

Stars ---------------------Angels

Candlesticks ----------Churches

<u>Revelation 1:20</u>

The mystery of the seven stars which thou sawest in my right hand, and the seven golden candlesticks. The seven stars are the angels of the seven churches: and the seven candlesticks which thou sawest are the seven churches.

A list of a few symbolism and their meaning. Remember, this form of symbolism is used throughout the Bible. The next "quote" is from Proverbs, Chapter 8, starting with 1st verse.

(1) <u>Doth not wisdom cry? and understanding put forth her voice?</u>

(**2**) <u>She standeth in the top of high places, by the way in the places of the paths.</u>

(**3**) <u>She crieth at the gates, at the entry of the city, at the coming in at the doors.</u>

(**4**) <u>Unto you, O men, I call; and my voice *is* to the sons of man.</u>

(**5**) <u>O ye simple, understand wisdom: and, ye fools, be ye of an understanding heart.</u>

(**6**) <u>Hear; for I will speak of excellent things; and the opening of my lips *shall be* right things.</u>

(**7**) <u>For my mouth shall speak truth; and wickedness *is* an abomination to my lips.</u>

(**8**) <u>All the words of my mouth</u> *are* <u>in righteousness;</u> *there is* <u>nothing froward or perverse in them.</u>

(**9**) <u>They</u> *are* <u>all plain to him that understandeth, and right to them that find knowledge</u>

The word "Wisdom" in the above verses is symbolic of a higher power, which could be "God" or "Angel of the Lord" or "Jesus Christ." They are all different names for the "Holy "Spirit.'

(**22**) <u>The LORD possessed me in the beginning of his way, before his works of old.</u>

(**23**) <u>I was set up from everlasting, from the beginning, or ever the earth was.</u>

(**24**) When *there were* no depths, I was brought forth; when *there were* no fountains abounding with water.

(**25**) Before the mountains were settled, before the hills was I brought forth:

(**26**) While as yet he had not made the earth, nor the fields, nor the highest part of the dust of the world.

(**27**) When he prepared the heavens, I *was* there: when he set a compass upon the face of the depth:

(**28**) When he established the clouds above: when he strengthened the fountains of the deep:

(**29**) When he gave to the sea his decree, that the waters should not pass his commandment: when he appointed the foundations of the earth:

(**30**) Then I was by him, *as* one brought up *with him*: and I was daily *his* delight, rejoicing always before him;

(**31**) Rejoicing in the habitable part of his earth; and my delights *were* with the sons of men.

(**32**) Now therefore hearken unto me, O ye children: for blessed *are they that* keep my ways.

(**33**) Hear instruction, and be wise, and refuse it not.

(**34**) Blessed *is* the man that heareth me, watching daily at my gates, waiting at the posts of my doors.

(**35**) For whoso findeth me findeth life, and shall obtain favour of the LORD.

(**36**) But he that sinneth against me wrongeth his own soul: all they that hate me love death.

I add this part of Chapter 8, Proverbs to show Wisdom was first recognized before the Heaven or the earth was created.

And from the book of Jeremiah, Chapter 4,

(19) My bowels, my bowels! I am pained at my very heart; my heart maketh a noise in me; I cannot hold my peace, because thou hast heard, O my soul, the sound of the trumpet, the alarm of war.

(20) Destruction upon destruction is cried; for the whole land is spoiled: suddenly are my tents spoiled, *and* my curtains in a moment.

(**21**) How long shall I see the standard, *and* hear the sound of the trumpet?

(**22**) For my people *is* foolish, they have not known me; they *are* sottish children, and they have none understanding: they *are* wise to do evil, but to do good they have no knowledge.

(**23**) I beheld the earth, and, lo, *it was* without form, and void; and the heavens, and they *had* no light.

(**24**) I beheld the mountains, and, lo, they trembled, and all the hills moved lightly.

(**25**) I beheld, and, lo, *there was* no man, and all the birds of the heavens were fled.

(**26**) I beheld, and, lo, the fruitful place *was* a wilderness, and all the cities thereof were broken down at the presence of the LORD, *and* by his fierce anger.

(**27)** For thus hath the LORD said, The whole land shall be desolate; yet will I not make a full end.

(**28)**For this shall the earth mourn, and the heavens above be black: because I have spoken *it*, I have purposed *it*, and will not repent, neither will I turn back from it.

And from the book of 2 Peter, chapter 3:

(**5)** For this they willingly are ignorant of, that by the word of God the heavens were of old, and the earth standing out of the water and in the water:

(**6**) <u>Whereby the world that then was, being overflowed with water, perished:</u>

(**7**) <u>But the heavens and the earth, which are now, by the same word are kept in store, reserved unto fire against the day of judgment and perdition of ungodly men.</u>

(**8**) <u>But, beloved, be not ignorant of this one thing, that one day *is* with the Lord as a thousand years, and a thousand years as one day.</u>

I list all the verses and Bible books above to give evidence of an age before the Genesis took place. We can now understand the first verse in the KJB, "In the beginning—" is referring to the start or beginning of this flesh age.

Throughout this book, I will call this Age, the 2nd earth age.

The second verse in our 'new beginning' has a wrong translation that needs to be displayed and corrected.

"And the earth was without form and void, and darkness was upon the face of the deep. And the Spirit of God moved upon the face of the waters." Genesis 1:2

The word "was" is the villain. The original Hebrew text translates this word as "became."

It's not much of a change, is it?" This little change made me start thinking; if God didn't create this earth 'void and without form', what happened to make it this way? Since this was a new beginning, I knew something terrible happened in the 1st Age, which unset

God. What was it? Could it have been Lucifer's rebellion? I've shown this rebellion took place in the 1st earth Age, and what were the results? God destroyed this Age; He destroyed everything; that is everything except his children.

My opinion, do you agree?

God's Spirit moved upon the face of the waters. Gen. 1:2

What is this water? Where did this water come from since God is in the creating process? The book of Revelation tells us 'waters' are people.

Rev. 17:15 states:

15And he saith unto me, The waters which thou sawest, where the whore sitteth, are peoples, and multitudes, and nations, and tongues.

Can we be assured then, if God informs us, "the waters" are peoples, etc., will this same definition be the same in the book of Genesis? I think so.

waters------People (symbolism)

So, I believe this water stated in Genesis refers to God's children; the good ones and the bad ones grouped separate. We are told the 'firmament' represents Heaven.

Jesus farther enlarges this concept in his parable of Lazarus and the rich man. In this parable Christ lets us know Heaven is divided into two parts with a vast gulf separating the good from the bad.

Then God said, "Let there be light." Genesis 1:3 Light dispels darkness, and the earth was in darkness.

Christ said, "I am the light."

John 8:12

Then spake Jesus again unto them, saying, I am the light of the world: he that followeth me shall not walk in darkness, but shall have the light of life.

John 9:5

As long as I am in the world, I am the light of the world.

Now you know why the world became dark at the crucifixion of Christ----because when they killed him, the light of the world was destroyed!

We can grasp our minds around the fact that Christ and the office of Savior are created at this time in history. He wasn't called Christ at this time, but the Angel of the Lord. A third of God's children had sinned by following Satan, and the rest were not so innocent.

Almost all of God's children need a sacrifice to pay their sin debt. A few of God's children are justified because they fought against Satan when he tried to overthrow God's Kingdom. The ones who stayed true to our Heavenly Father because they fought against the evil ones are called "God's Elect." These "Elect" are discussed in the book of Ephesians in the 1st chapter.

What is the next step in God's plan to save his children? Everybody knows when you leave a bad apple in the same basket as good apples, the bad will destroy the good ones. How does God separate the good from the bad?

Genesis 1:6
> And God said, let there be
> a firmament in the midst of the
> waters, and let it divide the waters
> from the waters.

Genesis 1:7
> And God made the firmament and
> divided the waters which were
> under the firmament from the

waters which were above
the firmament: and it was so.

Genesis 1:8

And God called
the firmament Heaven. And the
evening and the morning were the
second day.

God created a "firmament"
called Heaven. What is a
"firmament"? The firmament is a
division point or a "wall" or a "gulf"
as Christ gave in the parable of the
"Lazarus and the Richman." We
read in the book of Luke, chapter
16:26

(**26**) And beside all this, between
us and you there is a great gulf fixed: so
that they which would pass from hence

to you cannot; neither can they pass to us, that *would come* from thence.

The good sons are on one side of the gulf, and the evil ones are on the other side.

GARDEN OF EDEN

Trees as used in these verses are not the same as a normal tree a person would see in the forest today, but are 'Angels' or maybe better said, teachers. Evidence that I am correct is shown when the Tree of knowledge of good and evil, whom we really know as Satan, is given, and the Tree of Life are both in this Garden.

Symbolism

Tree of Life ----------------- Christ

Tree of good and evil -------Satan

God said Adam could eat (partake) of any tree except the one we are told is Satan. Why all the trees (teachers)? Remember, Adam has just been created! He has the mind of a newborn baby; he must be schooled or taught how to do the work God entrusted him to do in the Garden of Eden. Surprised, I said Trees represents people? In the Book of Ezekiel, we see a lot of different Nations and people are represented by various trees.

Ezekiel 31:1-18

(1) <u>And it came to pass in the eleventh year, in the third *month*, in the first *day* of the month, *that* the word of the LORD came unto me, saying,</u>

(**2**) <u>Son of man, speak unto Pharaoh king of Egypt, and to his multitude; Whom art thou like in thy greatness?</u>

(**3**) <u>Behold, the Assyrian *was* a cedar in Lebanon with fair branches, and with a shadowing shroud, and of an high stature; and his top was among the thick boughs.</u>

(**4**) <u>The waters made him great, the deep set him up on high with her rivers running round about his plants, and sent out her little rivers unto all the trees of the field.</u>

(**5**) <u>Therefore his height was exalted above all the trees of the field, and his</u>

boughs were multiplied, and his branches became long because of the multitude of waters, when he shot forth.

(**6**) All the fowls of heaven made their nests in his boughs, and under his branches did all the beasts of the field bring forth their young, and under his shadow dwelt all great nations.

(**7**) Thus was he fair in his greatness, in the length of his branches: for his root was by great waters.

(**8**) The cedars in the garden of God could not hide him: the fir trees were not like his boughs, and the chesnut trees were not like his branches; nor any tree in the garden of God was like unto him in his beauty.

(**9**) I have made him fair by the multitude of his branches: so that all the trees of Eden, that *were* in the garden of God, envied him.

(**10**) Therefore thus saith the Lord GOD; Because thou hast lifted up thyself in height, and he hath shot up his top among the thick boughs, and his heart is lifted up in his height;

(**11**) I have therefore delivered him into the hand of the mighty one of the heathen; he shall surely deal with him: I have driven him out for his wickedness.

(**12**) And strangers, the terrible of the nations, have cut him off, and have left him: upon the mountains and in all the valleys his branches are fallen, and his boughs are broken by all the rivers of the land; and all the people of the earth are gone down from his shadow, and have left him.

(**13**) Upon his ruin shall all the fowls of the heaven remain, and all the beasts of the field shall be upon his branches:

(**14**) To the end that none of all the trees by the waters exalt themselves for their height, neither shoot up their top among the thick boughs, neither their trees stand up in their height, all that drink water: for they are all delivered unto death, to the nether parts of the earth, in the midst of the children of men, with them that go down to the pit.

(**15**) Thus saith the Lord GOD; In the day when he went down to the grave I caused a mourning: I covered the deep for him, and I restrained the floods thereof, and the great waters were stayed: and I caused Lebanon to mourn for him, and all the trees of the field fainted for him.

(**16**)I made the nations to shake at the sound of his fall, when I cast him down to hell with them that descend into the pit: and all the trees of Eden, the choice and best of Lebanon, all that drink water, shall be comforted in the nether parts of the earth.

(**17**) They also went down into hell with him unto *them that be* slain with the sword; and *they that were* his arm, *that* dwelt under his shadow in the midst of the heathen.

(**18**) To whom art thou thus like in glory and in greatness among the trees of Eden? yet shalt thou be brought down with the trees of Eden unto the nether parts of the earth: thou shalt lie in the midst of the uncircumcised with *them that be* slain by the sword.

<u>This *is* Pharaoh and all his multitude,</u>
<u>saith the Lord GOD.</u>

The above scripture is another description of Satan and the reason God will eventually destroy him in the 'Lake of Fire.'

And also, in the book of Ezekiel Chapter 28, beginning with verse 1

(1) <u>The word of the LORD came again unto me, saying,</u>

(2) <u>Son of man, say unto the prince of Tyrus, Thus saith the Lord GOD; Because thine heart *is* lifted up, and thou hast said, I *am* a God, I sit *in* the seat of God, in the midst of the seas; yet</u>

thou *art* a man, and not God, though thou set thine heart as the heart of God:

(**3**) Behold, thou *art* wiser than Daniel; there is no secret that they can hide from thee:

(**4**) With thy wisdom and with thine understanding thou hast gotten thee riches, and hast gotten gold and silver into thy treasures:

5By thy great wisdom *and* by thy traffick hast thou increased thy riches, and thine heart is lifted up because of thy riches:

(**6**) Therefore thus saith the Lord GOD; Because thou hast set thine heart as the heart of God;

(**7**) Behold, therefore I will bring strangers upon thee, the terrible of the nations: and they shall draw their swords against the beauty of thy wisdom, and they shall defile thy brightness.

(8**)** They shall bring thee down to the pit, and thou shalt die the deaths of *them that are* slain in the midst of the seas.

(**9**) Wilt thou yet say before him that slayeth thee, I *am* God? but thou *shalt be* a man, and no God, in the hand of him that slayeth thee.

(**10**) Thou shalt die the deaths of the uncircumcised by the hand of strangers: for I have spoken *it*, saith the Lord GOD.

(**11**) Moreover the word of the LORD came unto me, saying,

(**12**) Son of man, take up a lamentation upon the king of Tyrus, and say unto him, Thus saith the Lord GOD;

Thou sealest up the sum, full of wisdom, and perfect in beauty.

(**13**) Thou hast been in Eden the garden of God; every precious stone *was* thy covering, the sardius, topaz, and the diamond, the beryl, the onyx, and the jasper, the sapphire, the emerald, and the carbuncle, and gold: the workmanship of thy tabrets and of thy pipes was prepared in thee in the day that thou wast created.

(**14**)Thou *art* the anointed cherub that covereth; and I have set thee *so*: thou wast upon the holy mountain of God; thou hast walked up and down in the midst of the stones of fire.

(**15**) Thou *wast* perfect in thy ways from the day that thou wast created, till iniquity was found in thee.

(**16**) By the multitude of thy merchandise they have filled the midst of thee with violence, and thou hast sinned: therefore I will cast thee as profane out of the mountain of God: and I will destroy thee, O covering cherub, from the midst of the stones of fire.

(**17**) Thine heart was lifted up because of thy beauty, thou hast corrupted thy wisdom by reason of thy brightness: I will cast thee to the ground, I will lay thee before kings, that they may behold thee.

(**18**) Thou hast defiled thy sanctuaries by the multitude of thine iniquities, by the iniquity of thy traffick; therefore will I bring forth a fire from the midst of thee, it shall devour thee, and I will bring thee to ashes upon the earth in the sight of all them that behold thee.

(**19**) <u>All they that know thee among</u>
<u>the people shall be astonished at thee:</u>
<u>thou shalt be a terror, and</u>
<u>never *shalt* thou *be* any more.</u>

We see here how Satan's reign will end; that is in the Lake of Fire. Also, we are given a lot of Symbolism to decode what God is describing.

Tyrus-----------------------------
Satan

Seas ----------------------------
People

Stone -------------------------
Angel

Mountain of God ----------------
Heaven

When Adam disobeyed God in the Garden of Eden, God placed a death sentence on all of Adam's children. It was a Spiritual death and the only way it could be removed would have to come from someone who loved God more than their own life or anything else in this existence. Abraham qualified to do this by believing in God and trusting God and was willing to make the sacrifice of his only son because God ordered him to make this sacrifice.

But what happened? God wouldn't let Abraham MAKE THIS SACRIFICE. Later, at the appropriate time, he would make the sacrifice. God would sacrifice himself in the form of Jesus Christ on the cross to pay the debt of sin Adam's disobedience brought on mankind. Genesis 22:7-13

(**7**) And Isaac spake unto Abraham his father, and said, My father: and he said, Here *am* I, my son. And he said, Behold the fire and the wood: but where *is* the lamb for a burnt offering?

(**8**) And Abraham said, My son, God will provide himself a lamb for a burnt offering: so they went both of them together.

(**9**) And they came to the place which God had told him of; and Abraham built an altar there, and laid the wood in order, and bound Isaac his son, and laid him on the altar upon the wood.

(**10**) And Abraham stretched forth his hand, and took the knife to slay his son.

(**11**) And the angel of the LORD called unto him out of heaven, and said, Abraham, Abraham: and he said, Here *am* I.

(**12**) And he said, Lay not thine hand upon the lad, neither do thou anything unto him: for now I know that thou fearest God, seeing thou hast not withheld thy son, thine only *son* from me.

(**13**) And Abraham lifted up his eyes, and looked, and behold behind *him* a ram caught in a thicket by his horns: and Abraham went and took the ram, and offered him up for a burnt offering in the stead of his son.

Chapter 2

I know what you're thinking; why are the rest of us being punished for Adam's sin and disobedience? God knew you would think and say this. So, to be fair, and God is fair, he gave this flesh age or 2nd Earth Age, 10 easy commandments to live by and not break. We call them the '10 Commandants', and so far, nobody in the flesh body has been able to keep them or maybe I should say 'not break one or more' of the commandants.

Enoch, of the old Testament probably came close because it is written:

Genesis 5:24

And Enoch walked with God: and he was not; for God took him.

The bible doesn't say Enoch was sinless; just say he pleased God.

And Elijah was taken to heaven without dying in the flesh:

2 Kings 2:11

And it came to pass, as they still went on, and talked, that, behold, there appeared a chariot of fire, and horses of fire, and parted them both asunder; and Elijah went up by a whirlwind into heaven.

These two are the only ones recorded in the Bible who went to be with God without dying a physical death. So, now for over 4500 hundred years, nobody has entered God's presence except these two. And you have the audacity to think God is unfair?

Now then, because God loves his children, he made the ultimate sacrifice by coming into this flesh age in the form of Jesus, the Christ. He did this to show us how to do it; and then, in the form of Jesus, he died on a Roman cross to pay Adam's sin debt and ours also.

More symbolism? Christ said he would teach by using parables only. Parables are a form of symbolism; or not?

Christ gave the crowd he was teaching a parable about the sower and the tares.

Matthew 13:24 and following.

(**24**) <u>Another parable put he forth unto them, saying,</u> The kingdom of heaven is likened unto a man which sowed good seed in his field:

(**25**) But while men slept, his enemy came and sowed tares among the wheat, and went his way.

(**26**) But when the blade was sprung up, and brought forth fruit, then appeared the tares also.

(**27**) So the servants of the householder came and said unto him, Sir, didst not thou sow good seed in thy field? from whence then hath it tares?

(**28**) He said unto them, An enemy hath done this. The servants said unto him, Wilt thou then that we go and gather them up?

(**29**) But he said, Nay; lest while ye gather up the tares, ye root up also the wheat with them.

(**30**) Let both grow together until the harvest: and in the time of harvest I will say to the reapers, Gather ye together first the tares, and bind them in bundles to burn them: but gather the wheat into my barn.

(**31**) <u>Another parable put he forth unto them, saying, </u>The kingdom of heaven is like to a grain of mustard seed, which a man took, and sowed in his field:

(**32**) Which indeed is the least of all seeds: but when it is grown, it is the greatest among herbs, and becometh a tree, so that the birds of the air come and lodge in the branches thereof.

(**33**) Another parable spake he unto them; The kingdom of heaven is like unto leaven, which a woman took, and hid in three measures of meal, till the whole was leavened.

(**34**) All these things spake Jesus unto the multitude in parables; and without a parable spake he not unto them:

(**35**) That it might be fulfilled which was spoken by the prophet, saying, I will open my mouth in parables; I will utter things which have been kept secret from the foundation of the world.

After Jesus finished teaching and went into the house, his

disciples came unto him and asked the meaning of the parable of the sower. This is what he told his disciples:

(**36**) Then Jesus sent the multitude away, and went into the house: and his disciples came unto him, saying, Declare unto us the parable of the tares of the field.

(**37**) He answered and said unto them, He that soweth the good seed is the Son of man;

(**38**) The field is the world; the good seed are the children of the kingdom; but the tares are the children of the wicked *one*;

(**39**) The enemy that sowed them is the devil; the harvest is the end of the world; and the reapers are the angels.

(**40**) As therefore the tares are gathered and burned in the fire; so shall it be in the end of this world.

(**41**) The Son of man shall send forth his angels, and they shall gather out of his kingdom all things that offend, and them which do iniquity;

(**42**) And shall cast them into a furnace of fire: there shall be wailing and gnashing of teeth.

(**43**) Then shall the righteous shine forth as the sun in the kingdom of their Father. Who hath ears to hear, let him hear.

So, you see, the multitude wasn't supposed to know the meaning of the parable, but Jesus' disciples were, and Jesus explained the parable to them. But there's more, I believe.

The children of the wicked one are Satan's children through mostly from the offspring of Cain from Lucifer's mating with Eve in the 'Garden of Eden'; Although this ended with Christ paying the sin debt of Adam. Now to realize this 'AGE' still has Lucifer's children roaming all over it, we should look at the mark God placed on Cain and his descendants.

But you might say, the Bible doesn't tell us what the mark truly is or was. And I say, Christ told us all things. As it reads in Mark 13:23:

But, take ye heed; I have foretold you all things.

If Christ foretold us all things; and Christ doesn't lie, where did he tell us about the mark placed on Cain? I say, in the book of Genesis; that is, if you can read with your spiritual eyes open.

Starting with Genesis 5:15 and continuing:

(**15**) And the LORD said unto him, Therefore whosoever slayeth Cain, vengeance shall be taken on him sevenfold. And the LORD set a mark upon Cain, lest any finding him should kill him.

(**16**) And Cain went out from the presence of the LORD, and dwelt in the land of Nod, on the east of Eden.

(**17**) And Cain knew his wife; and she conceived, and bare Enoch: and he builded a city, and called the name of the city, after the name of his son, Enoch.

(**18**) And unto Enoch was born Irad: and Irad begat Mehujael: and Mehujael begat Methusael: and Methusael begat Lamech.

(**19**)And Lamech took unto him two wives: the name of the one *was* Adah, and the name of the other Zillah.

(**20**) And Adah bare Jabal: he was the father of such as dwell in tents, and *of such as have* cattle.

(**21**) And his brother's name *was* Jubal: he was the father of all such as handle the harp and organ.

(**22**) And Zillah, she also bare Tubalcain, an instructer of every artificer in brass and iron: and the sister of Tubalcain *was* Naamah.

(23) <u>And Lamech said unto his wives, Adah and Zillah, Hear my voice; ye wives of Lamech, hearken unto my speech: for I have slain a man to my wounding, and a young man to my hurt.</u>

Ok, look down the list of names I have copied from the Bible. What do you see? A lot of begets. And what else? Do you read as I did the things Cain offspring were doing? They were all engaged in worldly object or making a life in this physical age. This is their mark! Nowhere is it mentioned that they believed in God or worshipped him. Could this be the reason Christ said, "you will know them by their works?"

Matthew 7:18 and continuing:

(**18**) A good tree cannot bring forth evil fruit, neither *can* a corrupt tree bring forth good fruit.

(**19**) Every tree that bringeth not forth good fruit is hewn down, and cast into the fire.

(**20**) Wherefore by their fruits ye shall know them.

And after Christ paid the sin debt on the Cross, the mark is on the whole age. The ones who are not Christ's seek only the things of the world. The ones who belong to Christ put him first and depend on him for their livelihood. Think about it.

Notice the symbolism in the above verses.

Tree ----------------------------- people.

Fruit ----------------------------- deeds

This 'Mark' will stay on all the peoples of this 'Age' until Christ returns and sets all things right again.

Eccl. 12:6

(**6**) <u>Or ever the silver cord be loosed, or the golden bowl be broken, or the pitcher be broken at the fountain, or the wheel broken at the cistern.</u>

Silver cord ------------------------- --Death

Golden bowl ------------------------- --Death

    Pitcher ----------------------------------
-- Death

    Wheel ----------------------------------
--Death

All the words given above are symbolic of death of the flesh body in the verse given above. And verse 7 also has a symbolic word. The word is dust; all flesh is composed of the dirt of the earth; and after life has departed the flesh bodies, the body will return to the earth and be dissolved back into it.

(7) <u>Then shall the dust return to the earth as it was: and the spirit shall return unto God who gave it.</u>

Dust ------------------------------

physical body

Revelation 15 and Deuteronomy 31 & 32

Revelation 15:3

And they sing the song of Moses the servant of God, and the song of the Lamb, saying, Great and marvellous are thy works, Lord God Almighty; just and true are thy ways, thou King of saints.

Deuteronomy 31:22

Moses therefore wrote this song the same day and taught it the children of Israel.

Deuteronomy 32:44

And Moses came and spake all the words of this song in the ears of the people, he, and Hoshea the son of Nun.

<u>Deuteronomy 31:30</u>

And Moses spake in the ears of all the congregation of Israel the words of this song, until they were ended.

Song? What does this mean? The bible informs us Christ's followers will be singing this song when they enter the Kingdom of Christ.

In our case, singing the 'Song of Moses' simply means we will know the contents of Moses' teaching by heart. We could sing if we choose, but we will be able to know the difference if someone or some group tries to change the verses.

Example: What did Satan use to tempt Christ in the Wilderness? Answer: Biblical scripture! Would you know the difference if Satan quoted scripture to you?

Matthew Chapter 4 beginning with verse 1:

(1) <u>Then was Jesus led up of the Spirit into the wilderness to be tempted of the devil.</u>

(**2**) <u>And when he had fasted forty days and forty nights, he was afterward an hungred.</u>

(**3**) <u>And when the tempter came to him, he said, If thou be the Son of God, command that these stones be made bread.</u>

(**4**) But he answered and said, It is written, Man shall not live by bread alone, but by every word that proceedeth out of the mouth of God.

(**5**) Then the devil taketh him up into the holy city, and setteth him on a pinnacle of the temple,

(**6**) And saith unto him, If thou be the Son of God, cast thyself down: for it is written, He shall give his angels charge concerning thee: and in *their* hands they shall bear thee up, lest at any time thou dash thy foot against a stone.

(**7**) Jesus said unto him, It is written again, Thou shalt not tempt the Lord thy God. Lord thy God.

(**8**) Again, the devil taketh him up into an exceeding high mountain, and sheweth him all the kingdoms of the world, and the glory of them;

(**9**) <u>And saith unto him, All these things will I give thee, if thou wilt fall down and worship me.</u>

(**10**) <u>Then saith Jesus unto him,</u> Get thee hence, Satan: for it is written, Thou shalt worship the Lord thy God, and him only shalt thou serve.

Jesus knew how to respond to Satan, the Tempter. Do you? Do you know which verses the Tempter was quoting?

Look in Duet. 8:3 for the first quote.

Look in Duet. 6:16 second quote.

Look in Duet. 6:13; 10:20 for last quote.

Be prepared! Study the bible; don't depend on some preacher to tell you what the bible instructs.

Chapter 3

The Song of Moses; biblical symbolism.

(1) <u>Give ear, O ye heavens, and I will speak; and hear, O earth, the words of my mouth.</u>

(**2**) <u>My doctrine shall drop as the rain, my speech shall distil as the dew, as the small rain upon the tender herb, and as the showers upon the grass:</u>

(**3**) <u>Because I will publish the name of the LORD: ascribe ye greatness unto our God.</u>

(**4**) <u>*He is* the Rock, his work *is* perfect: for all his</u>

ways *are* judgment: a God of truth and without iniquity, just and right *is* he.

(**5**) They have corrupted themselves, their spot *is* not *the spot* of his children: *they are* a perverse and crooked generation.

(**6**) Do ye thus requite the LORD, O foolish people and unwise? *is* not he thy father *that* hath bought thee? hath he not made thee, and established thee?

(**7**) Remember the days of old, consider the years of many generations: ask thy father, and he will shew thee; thy elders, and they will tell thee.

(**8**) When the most High divided to the nations their inheritance, when he separated the sons of Adam, he set the bounds of the people according to the number of the children of Israel.

(**9**) For the LORD'S portion *is* his people; Jacob *is* the lot of his inheritance.

(**10**) He found him in a desert land, and in the waste howling wilderness; he led him about, he instructed him, he kept him as the apple of his eye.

(**11**) As an eagle stirreth up her nest, fluttereth over her young, spreadeth abroad her wings, taketh them, beareth them on her wings:

(**12**) *So* the LORD alone did lead him, and *there was* no strange god with him.

(**13**) He made him ride on the high places of the earth, that he might eat the increase of the fields; and he made him to suck honey out of the rock, and oil out of the flinty rock;

(**14**) Butter of kine, and milk of sheep, with fat of lambs, and rams of the breed of Bashan, and goats, with the fat of kidneys of wheat; and thou didst drink the pure blood of the grape.

(**15**) But Jeshurun waxed fat, and kicked: thou art waxen fat, thou art grown thick, thou art covered *with fatness*; then he forsook God *which* made him, and lightly esteemed the Rock of his salvation.

(**16**) They provoked him to jealousy with strange *gods*, with abominations provoked they him to anger.

(**17**) They sacrificed unto devils, not to God; to gods whom they knew not, to new *gods that* came newly up, whom your fathers feared not.

(**18**) Of the Rock *that* begat thee thou art unmindful, and hast forgotten God that formed thee.

(**19**) And when the LORD saw *it*, he abhorred *them*, because of the provoking of his sons, and of his daughters.

(**20**) And he said, I will hide my face from them, I will see what their end *shall be*: for they *are* a very froward generation, children in whom *is* no faith.

(**21**) They have moved me to jealousy with *that which is* not God; they have provoked me to anger with their vanities: and I will move them to jealousy with *those which are* not a people; I will provoke them to anger with a foolish nation.

(**22**) For a fire is kindled in mine anger, and shall burn unto the lowest hell, and shall consume the earth with her increase, and set on fire the foundations of the mountains.

(**23**) I will heap mischiefs upon them; I will spend mine arrows upon them.

(**24**) *They shall be* burnt with hunger, and devoured with burning heat, and with bitter destruction: I will also send the teeth of beasts upon them, with the poison of serpents of the dust.

(**25**) The sword without, and terror within, shall destroy both the young man and the virgin, the suckling *also* with the man of gray hairs.

(**26**) I said, I would scatter them into corners, I would make the remembrance of them to cease from among men:

(**27**) Were it not that I feared the wrath of the enemy, lest their adversaries should behave themselves strangely, *and* lest they should say, Our hand *is* high, and the LORD hath not done all this.

(**28**) For they *are* a nation void of counsel, neither *is there* any understanding in them.

(**29**) O that they were wise, *that* they understood this, *that* they would consider their latter end!

(**30**) How should one chase a thousand, and two put ten thousand to flight, except their Rock had sold them, and the LORD had shut them up?

(**31**) For their rock *is* not as our Rock, even our enemies themselves *being* judges.

(**32**) For their vine *is* of the vine of Sodom, and of the fields of Gomorrah: their grapes *are* grapes of gall, their clusters *are* bitter:

(**33**) Their wine *is* the poison of dragons, and the cruel venom of asps.

(**34**) *Is* not this laid up in store with me, *and* sealed up among my treasures?

(**35**) To me *belongeth* vengeance, and recompence; their foot shall slide in *due* time: for the day of their calamity *is* at hand, and the things that shall come upon them make haste.

(**36**) For the LORD shall judge his people, and repent himself for his servants, when he seeth that *their* power is gone, and *there is* none shut up, or left.

(**37**) And he shall say, Where *are* their gods, *their* rock in whom they trusted,

(**38**) Which did eat the fat of their sacrifices, *and* drank the wine of their drink offerings? let them rise up and help you, *and* be your protection.

(39) See now that I, *even* I, *am* he, and *there is* no god with me: I kill, and I make alive; I wound, and I heal: neither *is there any* that can deliver out of my hand.

(40) For I lift up my hand to heaven, and say, I live for ever.

(41) If I whet my glittering sword, and mine hand take hold on judgment; I will render vengeance to mine enemies, and will reward them that hate me.

(42) I will make mine arrows drunk with blood, and my sword shall devour flesh; *and that* with the blood of the slain and of the captives, from the beginning of revenges upon the enemy.

(43) Rejoice, O ye nations, *with* his people: for he will avenge the blood of his servants, and will render vengeance to his adversaries, and will be merciful unto his land, *and* to his people.

(44) And Moses came and spake all the words of this song in the ears of the people, he, and Hoshea the son of Nun.

(45) And Moses made an end of speaking all these words to all Israel:

I gave you the whole 'Song of Moses' so you can read it and study it. Symbolism abounds throughout this song.

I'll give you a few of the symbols to help you get started and I think you can handle the rest.

God -------------------------------- Christ

god ------------------------------
Satan/anything loved more than God.

Jeshurun -------------------------
Nick name for God's children.

Rock ----------------------------
Christ.

rock ----------------------------
Satan.

Vine ----------------------------
what you believe.

Study this song; it could save your
eternal soul.

Book of EZEKIEL

Chapter One, Verse 4:
And I looked and, behold a
'whirlwind' came out of the North, a

78

great cloud, and a fire enfolding itself, and a brightness was about it, and out of the mist thereof as the color of amber out of the midst of the fire.

A look at the sentence:

First, the word 'Whirlwind' comes from the Hebrew word, "Ruach" and means "wind" or as used mostly in the old Testament, "Spirit". So, why didn't the translators use the word "Spirit" instead of "Whirlwind"? Could it have been because they could not imagine the way God could or would travel? Maybe, they could not picture the form of God in this flesh world. But we did learn in the book of Hebrews that God is a consuming fire! Hebrew 12:29. And Christ told us, "God is a Spirit". John 4:24.

But was this whirlwind the "Holy Spirit or not? Could it have been just exhaust fumes from the four aircraft that landed by Ezekiel?

Chapter one, Verse 5:

Also, out of the midst thereof came the likeness of four living creatures. And this was their appearance; they had the likeness of a man.

So maybe, we can conclude, God entered this flesh world in a cloud and brought with him the 'likeness of four living creatures' and these creatures looked like human beings. Were they alive or not; it does not tell us in this verse?

Chapter one, verse 6

And everyone had four faces, and everyone had four wings.

So, what have we seen? Something which looks like a man with four faces and four wings. Could this be a modern-day helicopter built in the shape of a man? The faces could be windows and the wings could be rotor blades; what do you think?

Chapter one, verse 7

And their feet were straight feet; and the sole of their feet were like the sole of a calf's foot: and they sparkled like the color of burnished brass.

Looks like we are looking at some type of landing gear, possibly a rail with padding on the bottom. The same as a modern-day helicopter. Obvious, the thing was built out of mental of some kind which sparkled and reflexed light.

Chapter one, verse 8

And they had the hands of a man under their wings on their four sides; and they four had their faces and their wings.

Personally, I think Ezekiel is looking at four vehicles currently. The 'hands of a man' could be door handles and I have already given an option for the faces and the wings.

Chapter one, verse 9 and 10

Their wings were joined one to another; they turned not when they went; they went everyone straight forward.

As for the likeness of their faces, they four had the face of a man, and the face of a lion on the right side: and they four had the face of an ox on the left side; they four also had the face of an eagle.

Do you recognize what Ezekiel is seeing? The symbols are the layout of the tribe of Israel when they camped in the wilderness after leaving Egypt. But each flying object carries these same symbols. Face of a man; "Rueben"; face of a lion; Judah; face of an ox; Ephraim; face of an eagle; Dan. These symbols are markings on these vehicles; Rueben on the front; Judah on the side; and Dan on the rear; Ephraim on the side. All symbolic of God's people.

Chapter one, verse 11

Thus, were their faces; and their wings were stretched upward; two wings of everyone were joined one to another, and two covered their bodies.

When the flying devices landed, he rotor blades were turned off and one set of blades were pointed straight up, and the other set were left in flying position or level. I am sure this gave the impression of covering the body of the flying device.

Chapter one, verse 12

And they went everyone straight forward; whither the spirit was to go, they went; and they turned not when they went.

Perhaps, you should visualize being in Ezekiel shoes; He had never seen a motorized vehicle before. All he was accustomed to seeing was cart being pulled by some kind of animal. So, when he saw a vehicle moving on its own and moving sideways or moving forward, he was astonished.

Chapter one, verse 13

As for the likeness of the living creatures, their appearance was like the burning coals of fire, and like the appearance of lamps; it went up and down among the living creatures; and the fire was bright, and out of the fire went forth lightning.

Keep in mind, the likeness of 'living creatures' was probably some sort of motorized carrier. Ezekiel was witnessing the exhaust of a motorized carrier with running light flashing around about. Nothing a modern-day helicopter would not have. The exhaust would seem like a super-natural event to Ezekiel who had never seen a flashlight or any kind of artificial lightning before.

Chapter one, verse 14
And the living creatures ran and returned as the appearance of a flash of lightning.

The machines moved so fast; Ezekiel could only compare them to a flash of lightning. Imagine what Ezekiel would think if he saw a dragster spin its wheels and take off down a drag strip with all the tire squealing and smoke and fire shooting out the exhaust.

Chapter one, verse 15 and 16

Now as I beheld the living creatures, behold one wheel upon the earth by the living creatures, with his four faces.

The appearance of the wheels and their work was like unto the color of a beryl: and they four had one likeness; and their appearance and their work were as it were a wheel in the middle of a wheel.

Do you remember the early version of hubcaps for cars? I am sure something of this sort was seen by Ezekiel. A full hubcap would appear as a second wheel inside a wheel.

I am going to let you finish the rest of this 1st chapter by yourself. The symbols are mostly repetition and I think you can handle it. Just keep in mind Ezekiel is trying to describe an object he has never seen before using only terminology of his present state in history. I think he did a pretty good job of it.

Maybe I should discuss the likeness of a 'throne' and the appearance of a 'man'. What do you think?

Chapter one, verse 26

And above the firmament that was over their heads was the likeness of a throne, as the appearance of a sapphire stone; and upon the likeness of the throne was the likeness as the appearance of a man above upon it.

In this scene, Ezekiel can see inside the cockpit and he sees the seat of the aircraft with a man sitting on it. Ezekiel visualizes the seat as a throne because he has never seen a seat of this type before. Visualize in your mind the way you might describe a modern-day passenger jet captain's seat if you had never seen one before.

Chapter one, verse 27

And I saw as the color of amber, as the appearance of fire round about within it, from the appearance of his loins even upward, and from the appearance of hid loins even downward, I saw as it were the appearance of fire, and it had brightness round about.

Imagine looking into the cockpit of a flying machine for the first time in your life. Nobody has ever seen one before or told you they even existed; how would you describe the object.

Ezekiel is probably looking at a man in a suit similarly to one worn by our men flying in a jet plane or an astronaut in a space suit. I sure the cockpit would have light shining and some blinking and maybe even a light to illuminate inside the headgear.

Chapter one, verse 28

As the appearance of the bow that is in the cloud in the day of rain, so was the appearance of the brightness round about. This was the appearance of the likeness of the glory of the Lord. And when I saw it, I fell upon my face, and I heard a voice of One that spoke.

In the cockpit are multicolored lights that have the colors of the rainbow and because Ezekiel has never seen anything even resembling what he is witnessing, he believes he is looking at GOD. Maybe he is, we are not told as yet. In the next chapter the pilot gives Ezekiel instruction to deliver to the Nation of Israel. This something impossible for Ezekiel to do. The Nation of Israel went into captivity 200 years before this event took place and have been disperse over the

Caucasus Mountains into what we recognize as Europe.

If the occupant was our LORD, he knows this, and I can see no reason for him to be talking to Ezekiel. If this is a messenger Angel from the LORD, it looks like he got lost somewhere along the way. Regardless, the message is just as real today as it was when it was delivered to Ezekiel.

In case you are wondering about the Nation of Israel; it is no longer in the old Palestine area. This Nation in the Palestine area on the East side of the Mediterranean Sea is the Nation or tribe of Judah. The old Nation of Israel is the United States and England and Europe. Believe me or don't, your choice.

I could keep going with the book of Ezekiel because it is full of symbols, but a commentary on this book is not my objective in this writing. I am picking parts of the bible where symbols could be given a meaning that is not correct or misleading. You will be on your own when you stand before the judgment seat of Christ. It will not do you any good to claim your 'preacher' led you wrong; the Bible is everywhere, and you are responsible for knowing what is written within it.

What I am trying to get across is to not take my word or any bible thumper's word for what the bible teaches; learn for yourself. Now a little more from the book of Ezekiel.

Chapter 28, verse 1& 2

The word of the Lord came again unto me, saying; Son of man, say unto the prince of Tyrus, Thus saith the Lord God; "Because thine heart is lifted up, and thou hast said, I am a God, I sit in the seat of God, in the mist of the seas; yet thou art a man, and not GOD, though thou set thine heart as the heart of God:

Tyrus is a Hebrew word which means 'Rock' or in this case, royalty. He is designated as a 'Prince', meaning one who waits to take over a throne and become King. He sits in the midst of the seas; there is a large rock off the west coast of the new Nation of Israel called Tyre. It is mostly a bare deserted place now, but in Ezekiel's time, it was a prosperous business place run by the Kenites. Kenites, as you should know are the descendants of Cain, the son of Eve and Satan. They never tried to do things

God's way but made their living off the world in commerce and trade. Anything to make a dollar; we still have them with us today.

Seas-------double meaning here. Midst of the people and also
a rock in the Mediterranean Sea

This part about the 'Prince of Tyrus takes up the first eleven verses in this chapter 28. It is God's judgment on the Kenites unless they change their ways and accept Christ as their King.

The rest of the chapter, verses 12 thru 26
deals with Satan, Lucifer, Serpent, Tree of knowledge, or any of his other names

or titles people know him by. Here, he is called the king of Tyrus.

Verse 12

Son of man take up a lamentation upon the king of Tyrus, and say unto him, thus saith the Lord GOD; thou sealest up the sum, full of wisdom, and perfect in beauty.

Verse 13

Thou hast been in Eden the garden of God; every precious stone was thou covering, the sardius, topaz, and the diamond, the Beryl, the onyx, and the jasper, the sapphire, the emerald, and the carbuncle, and gold: the workmanship of thy tabrets and of thy pipes was prepared in thee in the day that thou was created.

A lot of jewels and precious metals are given here. I am sure this list is given by God to show to the reader that nothing was spared in the creation of Lucifer. He was created perfect because of the job he was assigned to do. What was his job? He was one of the Cherubs whose responsibility was to guard the mercy seat of God along with another Cherub.

Verse 14

Thou are the anointed cherub that covereth; and I have set thee so; thou was upon the holy mountain of God; thou hast walked up and down in the midst of the stones of fire.

Verse 15

Thou was perfect in thy ways from the day that thou was created, till iniquity was found in thee.

Verse 16

By the multitude of thy merchandise they have filled the midst of thee with violence, and thou has sinned: therefore I will cast thee as profane out of the mountain of God; and I will destroy thee, O covering cherub from the midst of the stones of fire.

These three verses inform us to the nature of the covering cherub's (Saran)sin. Satan was among God's inner circle or the hierarchy in God's Kingdom. What happened? Satan became proud; that is, 'full of himself'. Instead of guarding the 'mercy seat' like his job called for; he wanted to sit on it as king.

This seat belongs to God (Jesus Christ) or as it reads in Isaiah 14:9 thru 12.

(**9**) <u>Hell from beneath is moved for thee to meet *thee* at thy coming: it stirreth up the dead for thee, *even* all the chief ones of the earth; it hath raised up from their thrones all the kings of the nations.</u>

(**10**) <u>All they shall speak and say unto thee, Art thou also become weak as we? art thou become like unto us?</u>

(**11**) <u>Thy pomp is brought down to the grave, *and* the noise of thy viols: the worm is spread under thee, and the worms cover thee.</u>

(**12**) <u>How art thou fallen from heaven, O Lucifer, son of the morning! *how* art thou cut down to the ground, which didst weaken the nations!</u>

(**13**) <u>For thou hast said in thine heart, I will ascend into heaven, I will exalt my throne above the stars of God: I will sit also upon the mount of the congregation, in the sides of the north:</u>

(**14**) <u>I will ascend above the heights of the clouds; I will be like the most High.</u>

(**15**) <u>Yet thou shalt be brought down to hell, to the sides of the pit.</u>

I am not sure who or what the stones of fire represent? My guess would be advisors or rulers for different aspect s of God's Kingdom. Remember, just my guess!

Continuing on:

Verse 17

Thine heart was lifted up because of thy beauty, thou has corrupted thy wisdom by reason of thy brightness: I will cast thee to the ground, I will lay thee before kings, that they may behold thee.

Verse 18

Thou has defiled thy sanctuaries by the multitude of thine iniquities, by the iniquity of thy traffic; therefore will I bring forth a fire from the midst of thee, it shall devour thee, and I will bring thee to ashes upon the earth in the sight of all them that behold thee.

Verse 19

All they that know thee among the people shall be astonished at thee: thou shall be a terror, and never shall thou be anymore.

Doesn't look good for the Devil or Lucifer or Satan, whatever name you know him by. Does it? These verses go along will what the book of Isaiah teaches. You don't have to fear the Devil; He will never rule Hell or anything for very long. Christ gave you power over him when he walked this earth in his physical form. Luke 10:19

God will destroy Satan in the 'Lake of Fire' at the end of the Millennium as it reads in the book of Revelation.

Revelation 20:1 thru 10

(1) <u>And I saw an angel come down from heaven, having the key of the</u>

bottomless pit and a great chain in his hand.

(**2**) And he laid hold on the dragon, that old serpent, which is the Devil, and Satan, and bound him a thousand years,

(**3**) And cast him into the bottomless pit, and shut him up, and set a seal upon him, that he should deceive the nations no more, till the thousand years should be fulfilled: and after that he must be loosed a little season.

(**4**) And I saw thrones, and they sat upon them, and judgment was given unto them: and *I saw* the souls of them that were beheaded for the witness of Jesus, and for the word of God, and which had not worshipped the beast, neither his image, neither had received *his* mark upon their foreheads, or in their hands; and they lived and reigned with Christ a thousand years.

(**5**) But the rest of the dead lived not again until the thousand years were finished. This *is* the first resurrection.

(**6**) Blessed and holy *is* he that hath part in the first resurrection: on such the second death hath no power, but they shall be priests of God and of Christ, and shall reign with him a thousand years.

(**7**) And when the thousand years are expired, Satan shall be loosed out of his prison,

(**8**) And shall go out to deceive the nations which are in the four quarters of the earth, Gog and Magog, to gather them together to battle: the number of whom *is* as the sand of the sea.

(**9**) And they went up on the breadth of the earth, and compassed the camp of the saints about, and the beloved city: and fire came down from God out of heaven, and devoured them.

(**10**) And the devil that deceived them was cast into the lake of fire and brimstone, where the beast and the false prophet *are*, and shall be tormented day and night for ever and ever

Lake of fire ------------------God is a consuming fire

Gog and Magog--------------East and West

Millennium ------------------1000 years

Resurrection -----------------brought back to life

4 quarters ---------------------whole earth

2nd death ---------------------death
of the soul and spirit

Beast ---------------------------
Satan or Satan's kingdom

Mark of the beast -------- followers
who believed in Satan

Since we haven't finished with the
book of Revelation, we will return to it.

Revelation Chapter one, verse 20
The mystery of the seven stars
which thou saw in my right hand, and the
seven golden candlesticks. The seven
stars are the angels of the seven
churches: and the seven candlesticks
which thou saw are the seven churches.

Seven is one of the scared numbers in Biblical Numeric and means the item described is complete.

(**16**) <u>And he had in his right hand seven stars: and out of his mouth went a sharp two edged sword: and his countenance *was* as the sun shineth in his strength.</u>

Stars ---------------------------------- angels

Candlestick ------------------------ church

Two edge sword -------------------- word of God

His countenance was as the sun shines in his strength. How bright is the sun? Silly question isn't it. We all know it's impossible to look at the sun without major damage to the human eye.

But Christ is the light of the world or so claims Genesis chapter one, verse 3, and we read: Sand God said, let there be light, and there was light.

Now you can understand why the world was covered in darkness at the death of Jesus on the cross. The light was put out for a short period; a period to signify he actually died.

But Christ told his disciples, he had the power to lay down is life and power to take it back up again. This he did that afternoon when he hung on the cross.

John 10:18
No man taketh it from me, but
I lay it down of myself. I

have power to lay it down, and I have power to take it again. This commandment have I received of my Father.

Chapter 4

Revelation chapter 4, verse one:

"After this;" meaning after he was given the message to the seven churches and he returned from being in the spirit when Christ first spoke to him: we don't know how long a time period took place, but later in John's life. "I looked, and behold, a door was opened in heaven: and the first voice which I heard was as it were of a trumpet talking with me, which said, "Come up hither, and I will show thee things which must be hereafter."

Where is Heaven? I believe it must be in a different dimension. Why? You might ask? I believe because there was a door to be opened to gain access to heaven.

Exodus 26:33
And thou shalt hang up
the vail under the taches, that thou
mayest bring in thither within
the vail the ark of the testimony:
and the vail shall divide unto you
between the holy place and the
most holy.

2 Kings Chapter 6, verses 15 thru 17

15And when the servant of the man of God was risen early, and gone forth, behold, an host compassed the city both with horses and chariots. And his servant said unto him, Alas, my master! how shall we do?

16And he answered, Fear not: for they that *be* with us *are* more than they that *be* with them.

17And Elisha prayed, and said, LORD, I pray thee, open his eyes, that he may see. And the LORD opened the eyes of the young man; and he saw: and, behold, the mountain *was* full of horses and chariots of fire round about Elisha.

Genesis 3:24

So, he drove out the man; and he placed at the east of the garden of Eden Cherubims, and a flaming sword which turned every way, to keep the way of the tree of life.

From the Garden of Eden after Adam sinned by disobeying God, there has always been a boundary between God the Father and physical mankind. You can call this dividing line whatever you care to name it; but I'm going with a separate dimension.

Revelation 4:1

(1) <u>After this I looked, and, behold, a door *was* opened in heaven: and the first voice which I heard *was* as it were of a trumpet talking with me; which said, Come up hither, and I will shew thee things which must be hereafter.</u>

2<u>And immediately I was in the spirit: and, behold, a throne was set in heaven, and *one* sat on the throne.</u>

The English translation says, "A door was open in Heaven..."; it could have read, "the vail was

lifted" or as John wrote after seeing
an opening into another dimension,
"I was in the spirit."

The bible tells us that when we
die, the 'spirit' returns to God who
gave it. Perhaps you didn't know
God places the spirit of one of his
Angels into every person born to
woman at conception.

Eccl 12:7
Then shall the dust return to
the earth as it was, and the spirit
shall return unto God who gave it.

Is this Old Testament
teachings only? What about the New
Testament teachings?

(50) Now this I say, brethren, that flesh and blood cannot inherit the kingdom of God; neither doth corruption inherit incorruption.

(51) Behold, I shew you a mystery; We shall not all sleep, but we shall all be changed,

(52) In a moment, in the twinkling of an eye, at the last trump: for the trumpet shall sound, and the dead shall be raised incorruptible, and we shall be changed.

(53) For this corruptible must put on incorruption, and this mortal *must* put on immortality.

(54) So when this corruptible shall have put on incorruption, and this mortal shall have put on immortality, then shall

<u>be brought to pass the saying that is
written, Death is swallowed up in victory.</u>

2 Corinthians chapter 5, verses 6 thru 8

(6) Therefore, we are always confident, knowing that, while we are home in the body, we are absent from the Lord:

(8) we are confident, I say, and willing rather to be absent from the body, and to be present with the Lord.

Job chapter 32, verse 8

But there is a spirit in man: and the inspiration of the Almighty giveth them understanding.

Do you need more proof? Would you believe Jesus? I know the English translation says, "born again", but the Greek manuscript says, "born from above".

John chapter 3, verses 3 thru 7

(3) Jesus answered and said unto him, Verily, verily, I say unto thee, except a man be born again, he cannot see the Kingdom of God.

(4) Nicodemus saith unto him, how can a man be born when he is old? Can he enter the second time into his mother's womb, and be born?

(5) Jesus answered, verily, verily, I say unto thee, except a man be born of water and of the spirit, he cannot enter into the Kingdom of God.

(6) That which is born of the flesh is flesh: and that which is born of the spirit is spirit.

(7) Marvel not that I said unto thee, you must be born again.

Are you wondering why Jesus gave his lesson to Nicodemus? Perhaps, the lesson was not really for him; maybe it was for all God's children who were being fooled by false teachings. Maybe it is for you who are just now reading this book. Maybe this lesson is for a mother who plans to abort their unborn baby and did not realize there were two beings in her womb. A new conceived flesh child and a spirit of one of God's angels being brought through this flesh age. Perhaps you are one of those persons who think or believe the spirit only enters a baby after they are born into this flesh age. Well, you are wrong!

Luke chapter one, verses26 thru 36

(**26**) And in the sixth month the angel Gabriel was sent from God unto a city of Galilee, named Nazareth,

(**27**) To a virgin espoused to a man whose name was Joseph, of the house of David; and the virgin's name *was* Mary.

(**28**) And the angel came in unto her, and said, Hail, *thou that art* highly favoured, the Lord *is* with thee: blessed *art* thou among women.

(**29**) And when she saw *him*, she was troubled at his saying, and cast in her mind what manner of salutation this should be.

(**30**) And the angel said unto her, Fear not, Mary: for thou hast found favour with God.

(**31**) And, behold, thou shalt conceive in thy womb, and bring forth a son, and shalt call his name JESUS.

(**32**) He shall be great, and shall be called the Son of the Highest: and the Lord God shall give unto him the throne of his father David:

(**33**) And he shall reign over the house of Jacob for ever; and of his kingdom there shall be no end.

(**34**) Then said Mary unto the angel, How shall this be, seeing I know not a man?

(**35**) And the angel answered and said unto her, The Holy Ghost shall come upon thee, and the power of the Highest shall overshadow thee: therefore also that holy thing which shall be born of thee shall be called the Son of God.

(36) And, behold, thy cousin Elisabeth, she hath also conceived a son in her old age: and this is the sixth month with her, who was called barren.

Why do we have a 2nd earth age or flesh age? The answer to that question is simple; in the 1st earth age or at the beginning of God creation after he created all his children, and the whole Universe, his children rebelled against the way God ran things. The arch-angel Lucifer believed he could do a better job than God. After all, he had been created the full pattern; he was more intelligent, more beautiful, had a bunch of followers, and he like being envied by so many followers. As it reads in the book of Revelation, chapter 12 verses 1 thru 9

(1) And there appeared a great wonder in heaven; a woman cloth with the sun, and the moon under her feet, and upon her head a crown of 12 stars:

Woman ------------------------ ----God's creation

Sun -------------------------- symbolic of God

Moon -------------------------- --- God's Children

Stars -------------------------- --- 12 Archangels

(2) And she being with child, travailing in birth, and pained to be delivered.

God had everything in place and was ready to push the "print button" so to speak; that is, to make all things permanent and fixed for all eternity when something unheard of happened, Do you know what it was? The bible will tell you.

(3) And there appeared another wonder in heaven; and behold a great red dragon, having seven heads and ten horns, and seven crowds upon his heads.

Red Dragon -------------------- ------- Lucifer

Seven heads ----------------- --- different offices

Ten Horns --------------Horns always represent Power

Seven crowns ----------------- -------- Royalty

> (4) And his tail drew the third part of the stars of heaven, and did cast them to the earth: and the dragon stood before the woman which was ready to be delivered, for to devour her child as soon as it was born.
>
> (5) And she brought forth a man child, who was to rule all nations with a rod of iron; and

her child was caught up unto
God, and to his throne.

Man child -----------------------
---Jesus, the Christ
Nations --------------------------
----Earth
Rod of Iron ----------------------
-----complete control

Lucifer was not alone in his rebellion of God's Kingdom. One third (about 10 angels) of God's children followed him. What was God to do about this rebellion? He could destroy the rebellious ones; but they were his children. Would you destroy some of your children if they disagreed with you? I didn't think so; and God didn't either. He chose another way; he destroyed that earth age and changed his angels into spirits. (Psalms 104:4) Hence, we are now in the 2nd earth age or flesh age. What else took place in 1st earth age?

(6) And the woman fled into the wilderness, where she hath a place prepared of God, that they should feed her there a thousand two hundred and threescore days.

The woman, God's perfect plan, was hid until such a time it could be brough forth again; that is after all evil and corruption has been done away. This will happen after the Millennium and under Christ's rule.

(7) And there was war in heaven: Michael and his angels fought against the

dragon; and the dragon fought, and his angels.

(8) And prevailed not; neither was their place found anymore in heaven.

(9) And the great dragon was cast out, that old serpent, called the Devil, and Satan, which deceived the whole world: he was cast out into the earth, and his angels were cast out with him.

So, the rebellion was put down; and God's Cherub, Lucifer or the Devil was cast out of heaven. And what about the one who followed Satan; they were cast out into the earth with him. So, everything is perfect now; right? Wrong; there are thousands upon thousands of God's children who were deceived or took part in the rebellion; what is to be done with them? Should God just go ahead and kill all of them? They are still his children and he loves even those who fought against him.

God destroys this 1st earth age, all of it, except his children who he changes into spirit form. God creates a new earth and a new heaven; a 2nd earth age or flesh age as we know it. He creates all the races and places them where he wants them on earth. Then he creates Adam and Eve and the 'Garden of Eden" for them to live in. They are to begin the process of bringing all the wayward children into this flesh age through the birth process and after they have lived a life time in the flesh, and learned about the love of God and accept him as their King; God will remove his child from the physical body and return his child back to live with him in heaven. This is what I believe; you may believe something different, that's ok with me.

But it's not all roses; because of what happened in the 1st earth age, this new creation will have to be tested. Hence, the allowance of the tree of knowledge of good and evil will be there (Satan). God gives Adam one command; "have nothing to do with this tree. Adam fails miserably! Because of this God places a death sentence on all who are born of woman. Now mankind will need a sacrifice to be made to God before he will remove this sentence from all mankind.

God, in the form of Jesus, will make this sacrifice on a Roman cross.

So, now, what happens to a person's soul or spirit when they die? A number of religions teach you either go to Heaven or Hell; depending on how a person has lived. Is this true? What does the bible say on the subject?

As I stated above, all souls go to Heaven when they die in the flesh. Is this fair; you could ask? Or maybe you should ask, Is God fair? I know you are wondering why a murderer or worse, if there is such a person, would get to go to Heaven along with a good righteous person? Think, now! Why would God bring all souls to Heaven when the flesh body which hosts these spirits dies? The answer: Heaven is where God lives and all souls have to be judged by God before they are sentenced. Just because a soul goes to Heaven doesn't mean Heaven is where they will spend eternity.

Revelation 20:12

And I saw the dead, small and great, stand before God; and the books were opened: and another book was opened, which is the book of life: and the dead were judged out of those things which were written in the books, according to their works.

There you have it; the reason all souls go to Heaven. They go to be judged. The fact they go to Heaven doesn't mean they will stay there. If you read my word closely, you'll notice the scripture said, "books were opened". Not just a book was opened. What books are we talking about; first, the book of life. Second, the book of works. I sure you are thinking; what are works and how do my works measure up to God's standard?

The book of life; what is it? How do I know whether or not my name is in it? Lost? Don't worry, I'll lead you through God's word until you know for certain where your name is or which book your name is in. Don't worry or wonder, your name is in one of the books, maybe both books. I hope your name is in both books.

First the book of life; your name in this book can only happen while you are still in the flesh; that is before your flesh body dies. You get in the book of life by believing Jesus Christ is the 'son of God' and repent of all the bad stuff you have committed in this flesh life. Then you must accept the sacrifice God made for you to pay your sin debt. Yes, sins cost and the debt must be paid. Jesus paid this debt by dying as a sacrifice to God for your repented sins. Don't be ignorant; God reads minds and can tell if you are repentant or not. Most people claim to repent of some bad deed they committed, when they are caught, when they really are just sorry for being caught and ashamed for their deed to be exposed. That's not repentance! True repentance comes when a person realizes what they have done is so hideous to even think of the deed makes them feel sick to their stomach. It becomes unthinkable in their minds that they would even do such a thing, even to the point of not wanting to look at themselves in a mirror.

2 Corinthians 7:9

Now I rejoice not that ye were made sorry, but that ye sorrowed to repentance: for ye were made sorry after a godly manner, that ye might receive damage by us in nothing.

2 Corinthians 7:10

For godly sorrow works repentance to salvation not to be repented of; but the sorrow of the world works death.

Do you understand yet? Repentance of a wrong means you won't commit the same sin again and nobody can force you to do it willingly. This is what it takes for Christ to forgive you and put your name in the book of life.

Alright, what about the next book; the book of works. Do you have good works? Your name is listed there; what does it say about you in the book of works?

James 5:20

Let him know, that he which converts the sinner from the error of his way shall save a soul from death and shall hide a multitude of sins.

1 Peter 4:8

And above all things have fervent charity among yourselves: for charity shall cover the multitude of sins.

Don't worry yet; you still have the Millennium to produce good works! Or do you? Perhaps you are wondering what a Millennium is or means. Basically, it means a thousand; as given in scripture, the Millennium would be a thousand-year span.

Revelation chapter 20, starting with verse 1

(1) And I saw an angel come down from heaven, having the key of the bottomless pit and a great chain in his hand.

(2) And he laid hold on the dragon, that old serpent, which is the Devil, and Satan, and bound him a thousand years.

(3) And cast him into the bottomless pit, and shut him up, and set a seal upon him, that he should deceive the nations no more, till the thousand years should be fulfilled; and after that he must be loosed a little season.

(4) And I saw thrones, and they sat upon them, and judgment was given unto them: and I saw the souls of them that were beheaded for the witness of

Jesus, and for the word of God, and which had not worshipped the beast, neither his image, neither had received his mark upon their foreheads, or in their hands; and they reigned with Christ a thousand years.

(5) But the rest of the dead lived not again until the thousand years were finished. This is the first resurrection.

(6) Blessed and holy is that hath part in the first resurrection; on such the second death hath no power, but they shall be priests of God and of Christ and shall reign with him a thousand years.

(7) And when the thousand years are expired, Satan shall be loosed out of his prison.

So, what do we have now? Christ has returned as he said he would. He has brought with him all who have died in the flesh from the time of Adam until Christ sets his foot upon the earth. And then what happens? All living people are instantly changed into spiritual bodies as are the ones Christ brings with him.

    1 Corinthians 15:51

    Behold, I show you a mystery; we shall not all sleep, but we shall all be changed,

    1 Corinthians 15:52

    In a moment, in the twinkling of an eye, at the last trump: for the trumpet shall sound, and the dead shall be raised incorruptible, and we shall be changed.

    Sleep ----------------------------------- --dead

    Trump ---------------------- beginning of a new situation

Raised -------------------------
brought to life

Incorruptible ---------------------
mortal brought to life
without fear of disease or harm to
physical body

How many trumps does the bible claim there are going to be? If you said 7, you are correct. So, the last trump must be #7. One more question, where are the dead? Did I hear you say or think "out yonder in a hole in the ground"? Well, if you did, you are completely wrong, we have already shown when the physical body dies, the soul or spirit (both are the same) returns unto God. So, what does God do with these spirits?

Remember the parable about Lazarus and the rich man? Lazarus died and was found to be in the bosom of Abraham on one side of a vast gulf and the rich man died and, where was he? O yes, on the other side of this same gulf.

Did you connect the dots? All spirits who do not belong to Christ are placed on the far side of the vast gulf where the rich man waits. What is he waiting for; he waits for judgment day! When will that be? It will happen at the end of the Millennium and it is called the "White throne " judgment and the ones who do not change their ways during the Millennium will be tossed into the lake of fire and eradiated.

Luke 16:22 thru 26

(22) And it came to pass, that the beggar died, and was carried by the

angels into Abraham's bosom: the rich man also died and was buried.

(23) And in hell he lifted his eyes, being in torments, and sees Abraham afar off, and Lazarus in his bosom.

(Hell is translated from the Greek word "Gehenna" and means a holding place and not hell. Gehenna was an actual garbage pit outside Jerusalem, and I guess Christ used this name to relate just how bad a place for spirits would be without God)

(24) And he cried and said, Father Abraham, have mercy on me, and send Lazarus, that he may dip the tip of his finger in water, and cool my tongue; for I am tormented in this flame.

(Tormented in this flame? Really Now, how can a spirit be tormented in a flame? Can you burn air? So, what flame can the rich man be tormented by? The bible informs us that God is a consuming fire. Hebrews 12:29 Perhaps, God was reminding him that he could have been on the right side of the gulf if he had made different choices. Your thoughts.)

(25) But Abraham said, Son, remember that thou in thy lifetime received thy good things, and likewise Lazarus evil things: but now he is comforted, and thou are tormented.

(26) And beside all this, between us and you there is a great gulf fixed: so that they which would pass from hence

to you cannot; neither can they pass to us, that would come from thence.

These, who are consider dead, on the wrong side of the great gulf are brought with Christ to earth when he returns at the 7th trump. So, there is still hope some of this group will make it. It all depends on their works during the Millennium or 1000-year reign of Christ before the great white throne judgment. Are you in this group? You don't have to be. Accept Christ as your savior and repent of your evil ways before it is too late.

Now I ask you a question; if there is no hope for a person to accept Christ after they have died in the flesh, why did Christ go and preach to the dead? What about the millions who have live in the flesh and have died in the flesh without ever hearing about Christ or the Living God? Is God so unfair that he would condemn these people to a fiery hell without them being given a chance whatsoever? I think not! What do the scriptures say? Or, have you been listening to a one-verse bible thumper all your life and are depending on his preaching to carry you to heaven?

1 Peter chapter 4:5 & 6

(5) Who shall give account to him that is ready to judge the quick (living) and the dead?

(6) For this cause was the gospel preached also to them that are dead, that they might be judge according to men in the flesh but live according to God in the spirit.

If there is no hope for mankind after the flesh is dead, why would Christ go to the dead and preach to them? What happened after Christ preached to them?

Matthew 27:52 and 53

And the graves were opened: and many bodies of the saints which slept arose,

And came out of the graves after his resurrection, and went into the holy city, and appeared unto many.

What graves are we talking about? Certainly not some cemetery out behind some church building. I ask again. Where are the dead? I tell you plainly; the dead are with the rich man in heaven across the vast gulf from where God's elections are enjoying the fruits of their faith. All, except God's elect were located there when they died in the flesh and went to heaven; only the part of heaven they were put in was not where God resides, but across the vast gulf where the rich man lived awaiting his judgment. You see, when Adam sinned in the "Garden of Eden", a death sentence was placed on all flesh men and women until a sacrifice was made to appeased God for the sin. Nobody in all the history of mankind did anyone prove satisfactory to God to make this sacrifice. Some came close, but close does not count. Finally, God chose to make this sacrifice himself in the form of Jesus on the cross.

Therefore, Jesus went and preached to the dead; there were quite a few spirits with the dead who accepted Christ and

had faith in him to rule God's Kingdom and believed him to be the savior. These were made alive and were permitted to leave the holding area where the rich man was and crossed the vast gulf and these are the ones who walked the "Holy City" located on the right side of the vast gulf.

Chapter 5

LAST DAYS ------------ARE WE
IN THEM?

2 Peter chapter 3, verses 3
thru 13

(3) Knowing this first, that there
shall come in the last days scoffers,
walking after their own lusts,

(4) And saying, where is the
promise of his coming? For since the
fathers fell asleep, all things continue as

they were from the beginning of the creation.

(What do you think? Is Christianity becoming a joke by most of the world population? Do the schools ridicule and scoff at anyone who even suggests a loving God created all things? Is anybody looking for Christ to return; after all, he been gone for about 2000 years and nothing has changed except for over population. Are preachers teaching their congregations to expect the return of Christ and how to look for the signs of his coming? I think not; but I just gave you two signs. Did you remember them?)

(5) For this they willingly are ignorant of, that by the word of God the heavens were of old, and the earth

standing out of the water and in the water:

(What did we learn 'water' was symbolic to mean? Water equals God's children, the good ones and the bad ones. Right? Remember in the book of Genesis, the good were above the firmament and the not so good were left below the firmament. The firmament represented heaven. Yes, I thought you remembered.)

(6) Whereby the world that then was, being overflowed with water, perished; (1st earth age.)

(7) But the heavens which are now, by the same word are kept in store, reserved unto fire against the day of judgment and perdition of ungodly men.

(Fire? Remember, God is a consuming fire. Hebrews 12:9)

(8) But beloved, be not ignorant of this one thing, that one day is with the Lord as a thousand years, and a thousand years as one day.

(9) The Lord is not slack concerning his promises, as some men count slackness; but is longsuffering to us-ward, not willing that anyone should perish, but that all should come to repentance.

(10) But the day of the Lord will come as a thief in the night; in the which the heavens shall pass away with a great noise, and the elements shall melt with fervent heat, the earth also and the works that are therein shall be burned up.

(A little confusion, I know. But we have two heavens to think about: one is physical, and one is spiritual. This verse scares a lot of believers; but think, when this happens, you'll be in a spiritual body. Nothing physical can harm you anymore.)

Remember Shadrach, Meshach, Abednego from the book of Daniel, chapter 3, verses 23 thru 25.

(23) And these three men, Shadrach, Meshach, and Abednego, fell down bound into the midst of the burning fiery furnace.

(24) Then Nebuchadnezzar the king was astonied, and rose up in haste, and spoke, and said unto his counsellors, did not we cast three men bound into the midst of the fire? They answered and said unto the king, true, O king.

(25) He answered and said, Lo, I see four men loose, walking in the midst of the fire, and they have no hurt; and the form of the fourth is like the son of God.

Back to 2 Peter chapter 3 verses 11 thru 13

(11) Seeing then that all these things shall be dissolved, what manner of person ought you to be in all holy conversation and goodliness.

(12) Looking for and hasting unto the coming of the day of God wherein the heavens being on fire shall be dissolved, and the elements shall melt with fervent heat?

(13) Nevertheless we, according to his promise, look for a new heaven and a new earth, wherein dwells righteousness.

So, Now I ask you, "How close is the end?"

Matthew 24:14, Christ speaking, (14) And this gospel of the kingdom shall be preached in all the world for a witness unto all Nations; and then shall the end come.

With all the television and radio and preachers worldwide, I say the gospel has been preached in all the world. So, the end of this physical world could end at any time. Or could it? There's one prophesy yet to be fulfilled. Do you know what it is? We'll find what has to happen before Christ will return in the book of Revelation.

Revelation 13:1 thru 9

(1) And I stood upon the sand of the sea, and saw a beast rise up out of the sea, having seven heads and ten horns, and upon his horns ten crowns, and upon his heads the name of blasphemy.

Sea -----------water --------------people

Beast -------------------------world power

Seven heads ---------------- different nations

Horns ------------------------ denotes power

Crowns ------------------------ dictators

Blasphemy -------------claiming to be God

This is what we are waiting on to happen. A world leader, claiming to be God, will rise from some Nation and will receive power from the dragon to take over the earth. This is the same beast we read about in Revelation chapter 12. The dragon we know is one of the names of Satan. Satan and his cohorts fought against Michael and his followers in the 1st Earth Age and were defeated. Now they will make one last attempt to overthrow God's plan for humanity. Will he succeed? We hope not.

(2) And the beast which I saw was like unto a leopard, and his feet were as the feet of a bear, and his mouth as the mouth of a lion: and the dragon gave him his power, and his seat, and great authority.

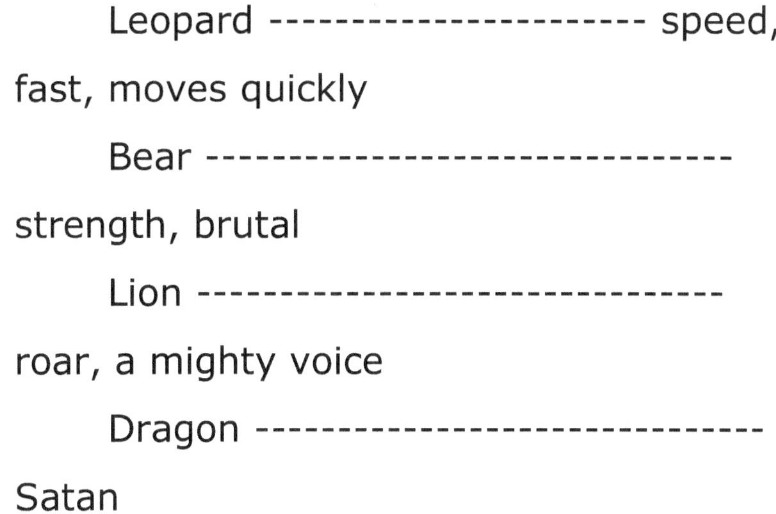

In theses end times, I believe a world power will come to the front and with the help of Satan will rule the world in a one world government. I could be wrong, but that's what these verses seem to be heralding.

(3) And I saw one of his heads as it were wounded to death; and his deadly wound was healed; and all the world wondered after the beast.

Question? Is the USA one of the heads of the dragon? If it is or if you think it is, did the election of Trump in 2016 cause a deadly wound to the beast? There are no wrong answers here; I just wanted you to think.

It is clear in my mind, had Trump not won the election in 2016, we would be in a one world system by now. What do you think? Well, anyway you look at the events of today, the Socialist party trying to overthrow the Republic of America was stopped; but the bible tells us the deadly wound will be healed. So, I warn you to play close attention to world events.

(4) And they worshipped the dragon which gave power unto the beast; and

they worshipped the beast, "Saying, who is like unto the beast? Who is able to make war with him?"

If you have a one world government, who can make war against you? Nobody, unless the war comes from inside the government or from some other solar system. So we can conclude the dragon is playing or pretending to be a great Spiritual leader. A leader who represents all religious factor on earth. The dragon (Satan) will assume this role. He will head up the government, the military, and all religious symbols. He will claim to be God! How will he accomplish this role?

(5) And there was given unto him a mouth speaking great things and

blasphemies; and power was given unto him to continue forty and two months.

(6) And he opened his mouth in blasphemy against God, to blaspheme his name, and his tabernacle, and them that dwell in heaven.

(7) And it was given unto him to make war with the saints, and to overcome them; and power was given him over all kindreds, and tongues, and nations.

We had a forerunner of this beast and dragon when Germany allowed Hitler and his Nazi Party to rule and make war on the rest of the world. Hitler was an amazing speaker and his speeches persuaded all peoples in Germany except the Jews. Of course, the Jews were sent to consecration camps and many died there. The next world ruler will not be killing people, just making the ones who oppose him look ridiculous in the eyes of the world until they confess him to be the Messiah.

(8) And all that dwell upon the earth shall worship him, whose names are not written in the book of life of the lamb slain from the foundation of the world.

God will allow this beast and dragon to rule earth for 42 months. Why would God do this? God wants to know who has done their homework; that is, who studied and believed the message God gave to them in his written word, the Bible. He told you what to expect; did you believe him? Are you going to worship the dragon?

(9) If any man have an ear, let him hear.

Does the Devil or Satan or the Dragon or the Serpent or whatever name you might know him by, have any physical children living among the peoples of the world? Yes, he does; they are called Kenites in the old Testament. Cain, from the "Garden of Eden" was his first child. Jesus referred to him in the gospel of John.

John 8:44

44Ye are of *your* father the devil, and the lusts of your father ye will do. He was a murderer from the beginning, and abode not in the truth, because there is no truth in him. When he speaketh a lie, he speaketh of his own: for he is a liar, and the father of it.

We don't hear much about Satan or Kenites anymore. After Christ paid our sin debt by dying on the cross and resurrecting back to life after three days in the tomb, Satan knows he has lost the battle between himself and Christ. All he can hope for now is to do what he did in the first earth age. That is, deceive enough of God's children into worshipping him; he believes that he can convince enough followers to follow him and God will not destroy him but will destroy this physical age and start over again. I personally don't think he has a chance anymore than a snowball in hell has. But we'll see, won't we?

I hope you do realize Satan is a spirit and has no physical substance now-a-days. It says in the book of Psalms and the book of Hebrews that God changed all his angels into spirits, and Satan is an angel of God, a cherub in fact.

Hebrews 1:7

And of the angels he saith, Who maketh his angel's spirits, and his ministers a flame of fire.

Psalms 104:4

Who maketh his angel's spirits; his ministers a flaming fire:

But before God changed the angels into spirits; what were they? Certainly not flesh and blood. No, they weren't;

but our flesh bodies are made in the same image. That is, the same food angels ate would also sustain a flesh body and vice versa. Remember in the book of Genesis when the Angel of the Lord came to visit Abraham before they continued to destroy Sodom and Gomorrah? Abraham killed a calf and fixed dinner for them, and they ate.

Genesis 18 verse 7 & 8

(7) And Abraham ran unto the herd, and fetcht a calf tender and good, and gave it unto a young man; and he hasten to dress it.

(8) And he took butter, and milk, and the calf which he had dressed, and set it before them; and he stood by them under the tree, and they did eat.

Psalm chapter 78 verses 24 & 25

(24) And had rained down manna upon them to eat and had given them of the corn of heaven.

(25) Man did eat angels' food; he sent them meat to the full.

Genesis chapter one verse 27

(27) So, God created man in his own image, in the image of God created he him; male and female created he them.

I gave you these scriptures to show a spiritual body and a flesh body are almost the same. Both can survive on the other's food. When Christ returns, don't worry about the food. A person in a spiritual body can eat whatever food is available.

Chapter 6

Question? Does Satan have any children in this flesh age? Yes! Are you sure? I don't mean the ones who act like your opinion of the Devil's children. I believe the bible. Do you? Let's read what the bible has to say on the subject.

Genesis 3:1 thru 6

(1) Now the serpent was more subtle than any beast of the field which the Lord God had made. And he said unto the woman, Yea, hath God said, Ye shall not eat of every tree of the garden?

(2) And the woman said unto the serpent, "we may eat of the fruit of the trees of the garden:

(3) But of the fruit of the tree, which is in the midst of the garden, God hath said, ye shall not eat of it, neither shall ye touch it, lest ye die.

(4) And the serpent said unto the woman, ye shall not surely die:

(5) For God doth know that in the day ye eat thereof, then your eyes shall be opened, and ye shall be as gods, knowing good and evil.

(6) And when he woman saw that the tree was good for food, and that it was pleasant to the eyes, and a tree to be desired to make one wise, she took of the fruit thereof, and did eat, and gave also unto her husband with her; and he did eat.

Serpent --------------------------- Satan

Tree of knowledge --------------- Satan

Touch ---------------------------- Sexual

Beast of the field ----------------- Other angels

Tree of life ------------------------- Christ

I teach that when Adam and Eve "ate" of the tree of knowledge (Satan), they in fact precipitated in a three-way sexual act. Eve became pregnant with twins, a child by Adam and a child by Satan.

When God came to the garden to visit Adam and Eve, they is from him because they had sinned by disobeying God's commandant. Adam said he hid from God because he was naked.

Genesis 3: 11 thru 17

(11) And he said, (God speaking) who told thee that thou were naked? Have you eaten of the tree, whereof I commanded thee that thou should not eat?

(12) And the man said, the woman whom thou gave to be with me, she gave me of the tree, and I did eat.

(13) And the Lord God said unto the woman, what is this that thou have done? And the woman said, the serpent beguiled me, and I did eat.

(14) And the Lord God said unto the serpent, because thou has done this, thou are cursed above all cattle, and

above every beast of the field; upon thy
belly shall thou go, and dust shall thou
eat all the days of thy life.

(15) And I will put enmity between
thee and the woman, and between thy
seed and her seed; it shall bruise thy
head, and thou shall bruise his heel.

(16) Unto the woman he said, I will
greatly multiply thy sorrow and thy
conception; in sorrow thou shall bring
forth children; and thy desire shall be to
thy husband, and he shall rule over thee.

(17) And unto Adam he said,
because thou has hearkened unto the
voice of thy wife, and has eaten of the
tree, of which I commanded thee, saying,
thou shall not eat of it; cursed is the
ground for thy sake; in sorrow shall thou
eat of it all the days of thy life.

I did eat --------------------had sex with Eve and Satan

Beguiled ---------------------------- seduced

Eat dust --------------------------------- -no more authority

Seed ----------------------------------- children

Conception --------------------------- --pregnancy

So, what do you think? Eve became pregnant; but whose children were they or better said, who is the father or fathers?

The bible states, God told Eve, He was going to multiply her conception and she would bring forth children in sorrow. We know Eve became pregnant and gave birth to twin boys, Cain and Abel. But here is where the confusion takes place in my mind, the bible tells us:

Genesis 4:1 & 2

(1) And Adam knew Eve his wife; and she conceived, and bare Cain, and said, I have gotten a man from the Lord.

(2) And she again bares his brother Abel. And Abel was a keeper of Sheep, but Cain was a tiller of the ground.

I believe at this stage in human development, I doubt Eve knew or understood where children came from or what caused them to be produced. Since God told her she would have children, naturally she would assume they came from the Lord.

What do you think? Your guess is as good as mind. The word "again" is derived from a Hebrew word meaning "to continue"; so, the verse should have read, Eve continued in Labor until her second child, Abel, was born; thus, she had twins. We know Eve gave birth to twins; but were they both by the same father or was each boy by a different father? Perhaps, you know, huh? The bible credits Cain as being the 1st murderer, but its not clear whose child he belongs to at the time of his birth. The apostle John has this to say about Cain, but is this enough? I think so; do you agree with me?

1 John 3;12

(12) Not as Cain, who was of that wicked one, and slew his brother. And wherefore slew he him? Because his own

works were evil, and his brother's righteous.

John 8:44

(44) Ye are of your father the devil, and the lusts of your father ye will do. He was a murderer from the beginning, and abode not in the truth, because there is no truth in him. When he speaks a lie, he speaks of his own, for he is a liar, and the father of it.

So, I'm going with the thought that Cain is the offspring of Satan and Eve. If you differ, that's ok with me.

By the word of the Bible, Cain had quite a number of offspring; is this how Christ could still accuse some of the religious leaders of his time to be descendant of Cain? Didn't all the peoples of the world die during the flood of Noah's time?

When you read about the flood during Noah's time, it seems there were only eight humans on board the ark. But is that right?

Well the Kenites made it through the flood. What is a 'Kenite" and why did I bring this subject up for discussion? According to the Strong's Concordance, Kenites are the name given to the descendants of Cain. The word in the Hebrew is Qayin and the translation given is, the name of the first child, also of a place in Pal. and of an oriental tribe, (Cain; Kenite).

I don't know why the descendants of Cain were called Kenites, but they were, and they made it through the flood of Noah's time. Conclusion: There were more people aboard the ark than it seemed, or the flood was not worldwide. Your choice? Why do I say this? Mainly, because the Kenites are mentioned several times by name in the bible after the flood.

You can find them listed in Numbers 24:22; Judges 1:16; Judges 4:11 Judges 4:17; Judges 5:24; Numbers 24:21; 1 Samuel 15:6; 1 Chronicles 2:55; and other places in the bible. I gave you these so you can readily see the sons of Cain, the Kenites made it through the flood of Noah's time.

How can this be; the bible only talks about Noah and his family. Or does it; how about this phrase?

Genesis 7:15

And they went in unto Noah into the ark, two and two of all flesh, wherein is the breath of life.

When we read this verse in the bible, instantly we picture male and a female animal walking side by side going into the ark. But humans are flesh also; could this verse mean a male and a female or all races entered into the ark with Noah? You decide; How else could the Kenites have survived the flood and also the other races living on the earth?

The other races, (black, yellow, white) are hardly mentioned in the bible and when they are, they are usually just called "gentiles" and they are bunched together. Have you ever wondered why? Well, I'll give you my opinion; the bible is about the story of one man and his family. No other peoples or races are mentioned unless they have a direct conflict with this one family. Which family am I going to name? That is an easy question. It is the family of Jesus Christ or I could say the family of God and his sojourn on Earth during this second earth age. Surprised? You shouldn't have been.

What did Jesus have to say concerning the offspring of Satan? Maybe you didn't know he knew about them. He told you about them in his parable of the sower. We'll cover this parable and maybe this way you will have a better understanding of the way Kenites work and how to watch for them. If they were of no effect in today's world, Christ would have omitted speaking against them.

Matthew 13:35 thru 43

(35) That it might be fulfilled which was spoken by the prophet, saying, I will open my mouth in parables; I will utter things which have been kept secret from the foundation of the world.

Foundation ------------------------- overthrow

World ---------------------------------- -age

(36) Then Jesus sent the multitude away and went into the house; and his disciples came unto him saying, declare unto us the parable of the tares of the field.

Tares ---------------------------------- Satan's children

Field ---------------------------------

- world

(37) He answered and said unto them, he that sowed the good seed is the Son of man.

(38) The field is the world; the good seed are the children of the kingdom; but the tares are the children of the wicked one.

(39) The enemy that sowed them is the Devil; the harvest is the end of the world; and the reapers are the angels.

(40) As therefore the tares are gathered and burned in the fire; so, shall it be in the end of this world.

(41) The Son of man shall send forth his angels, and they shall gather out of his kingdom all things that offend, and them which do iniquity.

(41) And shall cast them into a furnace of fire: there shall be wailing and gnashing of teeth.

(43) Then shall the righteous shine forth as the sun in the kingdom of their Father. Who hath ears to hear, let him hear?

Chapter 7

Notice, Jesus didn't describe the tares as Cain's offspring, but the children of that wicked one. Who is the wicked one? Satan of course and his children are the ones who believe as he did and follow his ways. Cain could be a distant ancestor of yours, but if you accept Christ as your savior and follow him and do things as he would do, you move from a child of Satan to a child of God. Simple isn't it? Not so fast, God reads minds and knows when you are faking it or being serious in your beliefs. So be careful!

Point in mind: When Jesus was discussing religious view with the Temple priest, he gave a good way to tell the Devil's children from God's children.

John 8:38 thru 47

(38) I speak that which I have seen with my Father: and ye do that which ye have seen with your father.

(**39)** <u>They answered and said unto him, Abraham is our father. Jesus saith unto them,</u> If ye were Abraham's children, ye would do the works of Abraham.

(**40)** But now ye seek to kill me, a man that hath told you the truth, which I have heard of God: this did not Abraham.

(**41**) Ye do the deeds of your father. Then said they to him, We be not born of fornication; we have one Father, *even* God.

(**42**) Jesus said unto them, If God were your Father, ye would love me: for I proceeded forth and came from God; neither came I of myself, but he sent me.

(**43**) Why do ye not understand my speech? *even* because ye cannot hear my word.

(**44**) Ye are of *your* father the devil, and the lusts of your father ye will do. He was a murderer from the beginning, and abode not in the truth, because there is no truth in him. When he speaketh a lie, he speaketh of his own: for he is a liar, and the father of it.

(**45**) And because I tell *you* the truth, ye believe me not.

(**46**) Which of you convince me of sin? And if I say the truth, why do ye not believe me?

(**47**) He that is of God heareth God's words: ye therefore hear *them* not, because ye are not of God.

Christ also said, "You will know them by their works".

Are we through with our discussion of the Kenites? I think so; are they still around today? Yes, of course; they are in all facets of life. This is the reason Christ said to leave them alone. He knows who they are, and the angels knows who they are, and Christ will take care of them when he returns. I just wanted you the reader to be aware they still exist today.

When will Christ return to this world? I don't know; nobody knows the exact time. We are told we would know the season.

Matthew 24:3 thru 44

(**3**) <u>And as he sat upon the mount of Olives, the disciples came unto him privately, saying, Tell us, when shall these things be? and what</u> *shall be* <u>the sign of thy coming, and of the end of the world?</u>

Notice: The disciples came to Jesus and asked him three questions; when would Jerusalem be destroyed? This happened in AD 66 by a Roman General Titus. Next question: What would be the sign a sign of his coming. Third question: When would the end of this world (aga) end? So, listen up as Jesus explains the answer to these questions.

(**4**) <u>And Jesus answered and said unto them,</u> take heed that no man deceives you.

(**5**) For many shall come in my name, saying, I am Christ; and shall deceive many.

(**6**) And ye shall hear of wars and rumors of wars: see that ye be not troubled: for all *these things* must come to pass, but the end is not yet.

(**7**) For nation shall rise against nation, and kingdom against kingdom: and there shall be famines, and pestilences, and earthquakes, in divers' places.

(**8**) All these *are* the beginning of sorrows.

Jesus gives you certain things which will happen. He said not to worry about them for they have nothing to do with his return. And history has shown us his words are true. We have had preachers and all types of con men claiming to be sent from God and people who claim they have the knowledge to get to heaven. One thing they all had in common; they were all liars for the most part. History has shown that there have been wars and such every century since Christ walked the earth in physical form. So, we should trust him to tell us about future events.

(**9**) Then shall they deliver you up to be afflicted and shall kill you: and ye shall be hated of all nations for my name's sake.

(**10**) And then shall many be offended, and shall betray one another, and shall hate one another.

(**11**) And many false prophets shall rise and shall deceive many.

(**12**) And because iniquity shall abound, the love of many shall wax cold.

(**13**) But he that shall endure unto the end, the same shall be saved.

Christian have always been slaughtered and hated for one reason or the other. It started with the Roman Emperor Nero who needed an 'escape goat' to blame the burning of Rome on and it hasn't stopped as yet. There is still reports of whole Christian churches being destroyed and all the congregations being put to death by forces who don't believe in Christ coming out of Africa and other regions.

(**14**) And this gospel of the kingdom shall be preached in all the world for a witness unto all nations; and then shall the end come.

Before modern communications were discovered, it was impossible to spread Christ's teaching and gospel around the world; but now, the gospel is easily heard around the world by TV or radio along with missionaries in almost every Nation. But the words of Christ ring true; but it is still not the end.

(**15**) When ye therefore shall see the abomination of desolation, spoken of by Daniel the prophet, stand in the holy place, (whoso readeth, let him understand:)

A little mistranslation here. The phrase "abomination of desolation" should have been translated correctly as "abomination of the desolator" stand in the holy place; meaning when Satan stands in the Holy place.

Daniel 11:31

(**31**) And arms shall stand on his part, and they shall pollute the sanctuary of strength, and shall take away the daily *sacrifice*, and they shall place the abomination that makes desolate.

I think you should study whole chapter in Daniel. I believe Christ means the conditions described in this chapter will be the same toward the end of tis age. The one world leader will start off professing one belief and change to a different belief halfway through his term. My opinion: what is yours?

(**16**) Then let them which be in Judaea flee into the mountains:

(**17**) Let him which is on the housetop not come down to take anything out of his house:

(**18**) Neither let him which is in the field return back to take his clothes.

Christ said, when you see these things happening, the end is right upon you. There will be no time to do anything but flee from the place where Satan sits and rules.

(19) And woe unto them that are with child, and to them that give suck in those days!

(20) But pray ye that your flight be not in the winter, neither on the sabbath day:

Being with child at this time in Satan's group simply means you are one of Satan's helpers and believe as he does. Gives suck means you are teaching the people to worship Satan.

(21) For then shall be great tribulation, such as was not since the beginning of the world to this time, no, nor ever shall be.

(**22**) And except those days should be shortened, there should no flesh be saved: but for the elect's sake those days shall be shortened.

(**23**) Then if any man shall say unto you, Lo, here *is* Christ, or there; believe *it* not.

(**24**) For there shall arise false Christs, and false prophets, and shall shew great signs and wonders; insomuch that, if *it were* possible, they shall deceive the very elect.

(**25**) Behold, I have told you before.

Christ will return as a "man-o-war"; he will put down all his enemies and sat his throne up and begin his reign as KING OF KINGS.

(**26**) Wherefore if they shall say unto you, Behold, he is in the desert; go not forth: behold, *he is* in the secret chambers; believe *it* not.

(**27**) For as the lightning cometh out of the east, and shineth even unto the west; so, shall also the coming of the Son of man be.

This verse needs a little help. It means as the Sun will come up in the East sky and shine toward the West, so will the Son of God come as promised.

(**28**) For wheresoever the carcass is, there will the eagles (vultures) be gathered together.

(**29**) Immediately after the tribulation of those days shall the sun be darkened, and the moon shall not give her light, and the stars shall fall from heaven, and the powers of the heavens shall be shaken:

The brightness of Christ's arrival will make the sun and moon seem dim in comparison. The stars falling from heaven simply means the bad angels will be kicked out from God's present.

(**30**) And then shall appear the sign of the Son of man in heaven: and then shall all the tribes of the earth mourn, and they shall see the Son of man coming in the clouds of heaven with power and great glory.

Why would people mourn at the sight of Christ coming? They mourn because they though he was already there. They have been doing Satan's work and worshipping him thinking he was the Christ. Now, they know they have been hoodwinked.

(**31)** And he shall send his angels with a great sound of a trumpet, and they shall gather together his elect from the four winds, from one end of heaven to the other.

(**32)** Now learn a parable of the fig tree; When his branch is yet tender, and putteth forth leaves, ye know that summer *is* nigh:

(**33)** So likewise ye, when ye shall see all these things, know that it is near, *even* at the doors.

(**34)** Verily I say unto you, This, generation shall not pass, till all these things be fulfilled.

(**35)** Heaven and earth shall pass away, but my words shall not pass away.

(**36)** But of that day and hour knoweth no *man*, no, not the angels of heaven, but my Father only.

(37) But as the days of Noe (Noah) *were*, so shall also the coming of the Son of man be.

(**38)** For as in the days that were before the flood they were eating and drinking, marrying and giving in marriage, until the day that Noe entered into the ark,

(**39)** And knew not until the flood came, and took them all away; so, shall also the coming of the Son of man be.

(**40)** Then shall two be in the field; the one shall be taken, and the other left.

(**41**) Two *women shall be* grinding at the mill; the one shall be taken, and the other left.

Two in the field and two at the mill; why would one be taken and the other left? Apparently both women were doing the same job and the two men in the field; weren't both doing the same job? It's what each believed; God reads minds and can't be fooled by appearances.

(**42**) Watch therefore: for ye know not what hour your Lord doth come.

(**43**) But know this, that if the good man of the house had known in what watch the thief would come, he would have watched, and would not have suffered his house to be broken up.

(**44)** Therefore be ye also ready: for in such an hour as ye think not the Son of man cometh.

When will Christ return? I don't know for sure and it a question people all around the planet would like to know.

Now then, Christ did tell us the season his return would take place, or better still, the events which would happen before his return took place. These events are what we are going to look at and study and see if we can come to some sort of time frame to expect our savior's return to happen.

When Jesus' disciples ask him about the end of this age, Christ must have been very worried his church (bride) could be fooled because he gave this same message in three of the four gospels and also, in the book of Revelation. In the book of Revelation, this subject is called the 1st seal and this seal is opened by none other than Christ. (Rev. 6:1 &2) This opening of the seals by Christ is basically the same subject I covered earlier in this study as given in the book of Matthew. In the book of Revelation, John is transferred into his spiritual body and enters heaven and sees things past, present, and future.

The bible states: and I saw when the Lamb opened one of the seals, and I heard, as it were the noise of thunder, one of the four beasts saying, come and see. And I saw, and behold a white horse, and he that sat on him had a bow, and a crown was given unto him and he went forth conquering and to conquer. (Rev. 6:1&2)

The book of Revelation contains a lot of symbols and if you are not familiar with what the symbols represent, you could have a hard time understanding what you read. In the verses above and throughout the bible, horses always denote power and strength when used in a parable or a vision. The bow given here and other places in the bible signify a weapon used by the person or persons in power to enforce their will on other people. I think we all understand the crown epitomizes government of one form or another. The word 'bow' is the correct translation; but the word is referring to the simplest fabric. The base root of the word is "tikto", a Greek word which means to produce from seed as a mother; it literally means to bring forth; to be born; etc. So, what we have here is a slight change of the simplest form in God's word being spread over the peoples of the earth.

Proof? Christ gave only one doctrine for a Christian. By the time of Paul, Churches were already dividing their belies. Some 1:11 thru 13said, "I of Cephas", some said, "I am of Paul", and etc. I see Satan's hand at work.

1 Cor. 1:11 thru 13

(**11**) <u>For it hath been declared unto me of you, my brethren, by them</u> *which are of the house* <u>of Chloe, that there are contentions among you.</u>

(**12**) <u>Now this I say, that every one of you saith, I am of Paul; and I of Apollos; and I of Cephas; and I of Christ.</u>

(**13**) <u>Is Christ divided? was Paul crucified for you? or were ye baptized in the name of Paul</u>?

Do you remember when Christ was tempted in the wilderness by Satan? What did he use to tempt Christ? Answer: He used scripture from the bible; but he changed the wording ever so slightly. (Matt 4:6) Look up the scripture in the book of Matthew and see if you can spot the error in what Satan quoted. Although Christ knew the scripture was misquoted, he didn't argue with Satan; but answered him with scripture. To save you time, the verses Satan quoted are from the Psalm 91:11 & 12.

The white horse given above in the 1st seal is supposed to represent Christ bringing forth truth; but the rider is a fake and is bringing forth a slight revision of the truth; just as Satan did in the temptation of Christ.

Now. I ask you, does your church preach and teach the true word of God? How can you be certain you are being taught the true word of God unless you study the bible chapter by chapter and verse by verse yourself, Knowing Kenites were the scribes taking care of the recording of God's word. (1 Cron 2:55)

(55) And the families of the scribes which dwelt at Jabez; the Tirathites, the Shimeathites, *and* Suchathites.
These *are* the Kenites that came of Hemath, the father of the house of Rechab.

On judgment day, will your preacher or Sunday School teachers stand beside you and explain to God you are innocent because they taught you wrong? I think you will be alone; your teachers will have enough to explain and answer for themselves.

The disciple John said in his epistle, "Beloved, believe not every spirit, but try the spirits, whether they are of God: because many false prophets (teachers, preachers) are gone out into the world." (1 John 4:1) So now, you can understand why Christ warned you about false teaching and doctrine: don't believe any man; not this man or any other, until you check him out by comparing what is taught to what the bible says.

What is the next sign Jesus gave us to be aware of before he returns? He said, "And ye shall hear of wars and rumors of wars: see that ye be not troubled, for all these things must come to pass, but the end is not yet," (Matt. 24:6)

In my lifetime, I have lived through two major wars and at least five police actions carried out in some part of the world. Hardly a day goes by without some talk about armed conflicts which could start a world war if something is not done to prevent these crises from escalating.

Christ said, "The end is not yet." So, you don't have to worry about any war bringing the world to an end.

The first seal is happening as I write and the second seal in the book of Revelation reads, "And when he had opened the second seal, I heard the second beast say, come and see. And there went out another horse that was red; and power was given to him that sat thereon to take peace from the earth, and that they should kill one another; and there was given unto him a great sword." (Rev. 6:3 & 4)

In the first chapter of Revelation, Christ is pictured as having a great two-edged sword coming out his mouth. We know the sword is symbolic; but what does it symbolize? In the second chapter of Revelation we read these words of Christ, "Repent; or else I will come unto thee quickly, and will fight against with the sword of my mouth," (Rev 2:16) Also, we find these words written in the book of Isaiah, "And he hath made my mouth like a sharp sword." (Isa 49:2)

Now, with these verses in mind, we can easily deduce the sharp two edge sword of Christ's mouth to be what he speaks   or teaches: in other words, the bible. Usually swords spoken of in the bible refers to the ability of a person to sway large crowds by their speech. As it is written in the book of Acts, Herod having this power. It reads, "and upon a sat day Herod arrayed in royal apparel, set upon his throne, and made a oration unto them. And the people gave a shout, saying, it is the voice of a god, and not of a man." (Acts 12:21 & 22)

It is readily discerned then from the above verse (Rev 6:4) and the other given verses that the great sword given to this rider is the ability to sway and deceive great multitudes of people with a religious doctrine that is very close to the truth of God's word; but with a little twist or a word changed here and there will change the whole meaning God's word.

Christ tells us, "For Nation shall rise against Nation, and kingdom against kingdom: and there shall be famines and pestilence, and earthquakes, in divers' places. (Matt 24:7) This verse goes with the verse in Revelation we are discussing and gives a clearer description of the "red horse" and the power given to it's rider to take peace from the earth and to sway Nations to kill one another.

As the rider of the "white horse" is a fake teacher who imitates Christ; so is the rider of the "red horse" who preaches peace through war and one world government.

Satan is the rider on both horses. Just different ways he is trying to take over the world.

"All these are the beginning of sorrows", said Christ to his disciples. This word "sorrow" comes from the Greek word "odin" and literary means "a pang" like in childbirth; in other words Christ is letting us know when we see these signs come about, they will come faster and faster until the end of this age is over.

Christ then tells his disciples his people will be persecuted and hated and killed through all the wars. He said many would "stumble" and "betray one another" and many "false prophets" would come forth. And because of iniquity, the love of many would grow cold. (Matt 24:9 thru 12) What love is this? The love of Christ and the truth of his gospel; many will listen to the false teaching and Christ will say to them when he returns, "I never knew you." (Matt 7;23)

Now, we look to the future events which will cumulate in the return of Christ. The next sign given by Christ, "when ye therefore shall see the "abomination of desolation", spoken of by Daniel the prophet, stand in the holy place, (whoso reads, let him understand). At this point, Christ broke off his prophecies and gave us several warnings for us to remember. We'll take a look at Christ's words or statements one at a time and see if we can come to a conclusion of the future events to take place.

First, the "abomination of desolation" needs to be understood.

English grammar helps us understand an event cannot stand on its own since it has no way to move about without help; so, the wording must be off. Moffett's bible gives the translation to be "abomination of the desolator". And I tend to agree with him. Who is the desolator? He can be no other than Satan since the name given for this person in the book of Revelation translated from the Greek is "Apollon", which means "the destroyer".

Christ said he would stand in the holy place, which means God's earthly throne located on Mount Zion inside Jerusalem on the North side. (Psalm 48) When you see Satan standing there in the holy place, you can be assured the end is just around the corner so to speak.

Since Christ told us the "abomination of desolation" was spoken by Daniel the prophet, let's search the book of Daniel and see if we can understand Christ's words. We have five places in the book of Daniel which mentions the "abomination of desolation", and I'll give them to you in order. The first time is in Daniel 8:13 and reads, "how long shall be the vision concerning the daily sacrifice, and the transgression of desolation, to yield both the sanctuary and the host to be trodden under foot?" This verse tells us where it will take place but not what it is.

Now we'll look at the next place it is mentioned in the book of Daniel. We'll find it in Danie; 9:27 and it reads, "And he shall confirm the covenant with many for one week: (7 years) and in the midst of the week, (3 & 1/2 years) he (Satan) shall cause the sacrifice and the oblation to ease, and for the over spreading of abominations, he shall make it desolate, even until the consummation, and that determined shall be poured determined shall be poured upon the desolate." (desolator) In this verse we have the meaning of the abomination of desolation; in other words, Satan will start his rule play acting as the returned Christ, but when he has consolidated his power worldwide, he will do away with the sacraments of worship God commanded his people to do forever. This would include the "Lord's Supper, Baptism, and teaching the bible, etc."

Again, in Daniel 11:31, we have reference to the abomination that makes desolate, and the verse reads, "And arms shall stand on his (Satan) part, and they shall pollute the sanctuary of strength, and shall take away the daily sacrifice, and they shall place the abomination that makes desolate."; Take notice, the verse informs us "arms shall stand on his part"; which is to say he will have all military help needed to have his will obeyed by this time. What is a Christian's daily sacrifice other then Christ who died for the repented sinner so now we can go directly to God to ask for his blessing and protection? Satan will do away with prayer to God because he will insist the people can now pray to him because he will claim to be the returned Christ. This why he is called the "Anti-Christ". The correct translation is "Instead of Christ".

And the last place is Daniel 12:11, and it reads, "And from the time that the daily sacrifice shall be taken away, and the abomination that makes desolate set up, there shall be a thousand two hundred and ninety days." Now this verse gives us a time frame we can use to do some figuring. Since the exact year of Satan's reign hasn't been established since his coming is still in the future, we'll have to wait for some things to happen before we can guess Christ's return. These numbers will only give us the "season" of Christ's return, anyway. All I can say is when Satan begins his rule; after 3½ years, he will claim to be King over all the earth.

Then, there will be a great tribulation; only one catch, this is Satan's tribulation, or the time when he begins to round up all God's elect who have refused to bow a knee to him. It's going to be a tough time, but God knows his elect can stand the test of

who is the real Christ and when they are bought before Satan, the Holy Spirit will speak through them as a witness to the whole world. (Luke 12:11-12)

Chapter 8

Our main clue to the return of Christ is given in 2 Thessalonians, chapter 2, and it reads, "Now we beseech you brethren, by the coming of our Lord Jesus Christ, and by our gathering together unto him. That ye be not soon shaken in mind, or be troubled, neither by spirit nor by word, nor by letter as from us, as that the day of Christ is at hand. Let no man deceive you by any means: for that day shall not come except there come a falling away first, and that man os sin be revealed, the son of perdition; who opposes and exalts himself above all that is worshipped; so that he as God sits in the temple of God, showing himself that he is God." (2 Thess 2:1-4)

Who is this man of Sin? It can be no other then Satan himself; he is the only one who has been sentenced to death by name in the entire bible. (Eze 28:18-19)

What about this falling away first? Do you understand what this phrase means? Listen up now; when Satan arrives on Mount Zion, People will be dumbfounded at how handsome the devil will be and will be acting in the role of Jesus and be so convincing that, "all the world will whore after the beast", except God's elect whose names are written in the Lamb's book of Life.

Christ will return at the 7th trump. But, he may not come as you would expect or have been taught. Why do I say this? Jesus gives us an example of the way situations can change.

Mattthew11:10-15

(**10**) For this is *he*, of whom it is written, Behold, I send my messenger before thy face, which shall prepare thy way before thee.

(**11**) Verily I say unto you, among them that are born of women there hath not risen a greater than John the Baptist: notwithstanding he that is least in the kingdom of heaven is greater than he.

(**12**) And from the days of John the Baptist until now the kingdom of heaven suffereth violence, and the violent take it by force.

(**13)** For all the prophets and the law prophesied until John.

(**14)** And if ye will receive *it*, this is Elias, which was for to come.   (Elias; Greek -------------Elijah; Hebrew)

(**15)** He that hath ears to hear, let him hear.

I threw this in so if the end of this world and the coming of Christ is not 100% as the bible writes, be aware of in "like manner."

RAPTURE

RAPTURE? Is this doctrine true or false?

The word "rapture" is not in the bible; but is this a true event? Let's take a little time and see if we can find the truth?

I purposely waited to comment on the "so-called" Rapture Doctrine until I was the end of this book. I know a lot of my readers will not agree with what is printed here, and that's alright with me; but is it alright with God?

First, let me say this before you close this book and wish you had your money back. The word "Rapture" isn't in the bible or in any ancient manuscripts. So why and how did this doctrine surface to the public?

It started with a 15-year-old girl by name of Margaret McDonald, a young girl who lived at Glasgow, Scotland, who claimed to have had a vision of the end times.

Margaret's Revelation

"It was first the awful state of the land that was pressed upon me. I saw the blindness and infatuation of the people to be very great. I felt the cry of Liberty just to be the hiss of the serpent, to drown them in perdition. It was just 'no God.' I repeated the words, Now there is distress of nations, with perplexity, the seas and the waves roaring, men's hearts failing them for fear. Now look out for the sign of the Son of Man. Here I was made to stop and cry out, O it is not known what the sign of the Son of Man is; the people of God think they are waiting, but they know not what it is. I felt this needed to be

revealed, and that there was great darkness and error about it; but suddenly what it was burst upon me with a glorious light. I saw it was just the Lord himself descending from Heaven with a shout, just the glorified man, even Jesus; but that all must, as Stephen was, be filled with the Holy Ghost, that they might look up, and see the brightness of the Father's glory. I saw the error to be, that men think that it will be something seen by the natural eye; but 'tis spiritual discernment that is needed, the eye of God in his people. Many passages were revealed, in a light in which I had not before seen them. I repeated, 'Now is the kingdom of Heaven like unto ten virgins, who went forth to meet the Bridegroom, five wise and five foolish; they that were foolish took their lamps, but took no oil with them; but they that were wise took oil in their vessels with their lamps.' 'But be ye not unwise, but understanding what the will of the Lord is; and be not drunk with wine wherein is excess, but be filled with the Spirit.' This was the oil the wise virgins took in their vessels – this is the light to be kept burning – the light of God – that we may discern that which cometh not with observation to the natural eye. Only those who have the light of God within them will see the sign of his appearance. No need to follow them who say, see here, or see there, for his day shall be as the lightning to those in whom the living Christ is. 'Tis Christ in us that will lift us up – he is the light – 'tis only those that are alive in him that will be caught up to meet him in the air. I saw that we must be in the Spirit, that we might see spiritual things. John was in the Spirit, when he saw a throne set in Heaven. But I saw that the glory of the ministration of the Spirit had not been known. I repeated frequently, but the spiritual temple must and shall be reared, and the fullness of Christ be poured into his body, and then shall we be caught up to meet him. Oh none will be counted worthy of this calling but his body, which is the church, and which must be a candlestick all of gold. I often said, Oh the glorious inbreaking of God which is now about to burst on this earth; Oh the glorious temple which is now about to be reared, the bride adorned for her husband; and Oh what a holy, holy bride she must he, to be prepared for such a glorious bridegroom. I said, Now shall the people of God have to do with realities – now shall the glorious mystery of God in our nature be known – now shall it be known what it is for man to be glorified. I felt that the revelation of Jesus Christ had yet to be opened up – it is not knowledge about God that it contains, but it is an entering into God – I saw that there was a glorious breaking in of God to be. I felt as Elijah, surrounded with chariots of fire. I saw as it were, the spiritual temple reared, and the Head Stone brought forth with shoutings of grace, grace, unto it. It was a glorious light above the brightness of the sun that shone round about me. I felt that those who were filled with the Spirit could see spiritual things, and feel walking in the midst of them, while those who had not the Spirit could see nothing – so that two shall be in one bed, the one taken and the other left, because the one has the light of God within while the other cannot see the Kingdom of Heaven. I saw the people of God in an awfully dangerous situation, surrounded by nets and entanglements, about to be tried, and many about to be deceived and fall. Now will THE WICKED be revealed, with all power and signs and lying wonders, so that it it was possible the very elect will be deceived – This is the fiery trial which is to try us. – It will be for the purging and purifying of the real members of the body of Jesus; but Oh it will be a fiery trial. Every soul will he shaken to the very centre. The enemy will try to shake in everything we have believed – but the trial of real faith will be found to honour and praise and glory. Nothing but what is of God will stand. The stony-ground hearers will be made manifest – the love of many will wax cold.

I frequently said that night, and often since, now shall the awful sight of a false Christ be seen on this earth, and nothing but the living Christ in us can detect this awful attempt of the enemy to deceive – for it is with all deceivableness of unrighteousness he will work – he will have a counterpart for every part of God's truth, and an imitation for every work of the Spirit. The Spirit must and will be poured out on the church, that she may be purified and filled with God – and just in proportion as the Spirit of God works, so will he – when our Lord anoints men with power, so will he. This is particularly the nature of the trial, through which those are to pass who will be counted worthy to stand before the

*Son of man. There will he outward trial
too, but 'tis principally temptation. It is
brought on by the outpouring of the
Spirit, and will just increase in proportion
as the Spirit is poured out. The trial of
the Church is from Antichrist. It is by
being filled with the Spirit that we shall
be kept. I frequently said, Oh be filled
with the Spirit – have the light of God in
you, that you may detect Satan – be full
of eyes within -be clay in the hands of
the potter -submit to be filled, filled with
God. This will build the temple. It is not
by might nor by power, but by my Spirit,
saith the Lord. This will fit us to enter
into the marriage supper of the Lamb. I
saw it to be the will of God that all should
be filled. But what hindered the real life
of God from being received by his people,
was their turning from Jesus, who is the*

an outpouring of the Spirit on the body, such as has not been, a baptism of fire, that all the dross may be put away. Oh there must and will be such an indwelling of the living God as has not been – the servants of God sealed in their foreheads – great conformity to Jesus – his holy holy image seen in his people – just the bride made comely by his comeliness put upon her. This is what we are at present made to pray much for, that speedily we may all be made ready to meet our Lord in the air – and it will be. Jesus wants his bride. His desire is toward us. He that shall come, will come, and will not tarry. Amen and Amen Even so come Lord Jesus."

END OF MARAGARET MCDONALD vision

This vision is where it all started; a couple of preachers heard of this vision and started preaching the "rapture theory" and like most things of a worldly nature, this new idea found a lot of willing ears.

But don't listen to me; what does the bible say about a fly away doctrine?

Ezekiel 13:20

(20) Wherefore thus saith the Lord God; Behold, I am against your pillars, where with ye there hunt the souls to make them fly, and I will tear them from your arms, and will let the souls go, even the souls that ye hunt to make them fly.

What else do I need to say on the subject? The apostle Paul explained the subject pretty good in his writing to the

1 Thess. 3:16-17

(**16**) For the Lord himself shall descend from heaven with a shout, with the voice of the archangel, and with the trump of God: and the dead in Christ shall rise first:

(**17**) Then we which are alive *and* remain shall be caught up together with them in the clouds, to meet the Lord in the air: and so shall we ever be with the Lord.

The dead in Christ will rise first. Why? Simply, because all people go to heaven when they die as explained in Eccl 12:6-7

Eccl 12:6 & 7

(**6**) <u>Or ever the silver cord be loosed, or the golden bowl be broken, or the pitcher be broken at the fountain, or the wheel broken at the cistern.</u>

(**7**) <u>Then shall the dust return to the earth as it was: and the spirit shall return unto God who gave it.</u>

Silver cord be loosed, or the golden bowl be broken, or the pitcher be broken at the fountain, or the wheel broken at the cistern, are all poetic expressions meaning when this flesh body dies.

All go to heaven when they die; the good, the bad, and even the ugly. Why? Only God is the judge; God lives in

Heaven and nobody goes to hell until they have had a trial before God.

Oh, they don't get the joys heaven has to offer, but are placed across the vast gulf with the "rich man" as the parable Jesus gave. Didn't realize there are two parts to heaven? Well, now you know.

Chapter 10

Since I started talking about 'end times', let take a look at some of the things God has said will take place in this flesh age before the end of this age ends and Jesus the Christ will return and make all things right.

There are a quite a few symbols in the book of Daniel and which helps the average person understand the book of Revelation.

In the book od Daniel, in chapter 2, we have a King who has had a dream, but cannot remember the dream; he just knows he has had one and it puzzles him to know the dream and the meaning. God gives Daniel the answer to the King's request, but the dream is really for the end time of this flesh age.

Daniel 2:28

28But there is a God in heaven that revealeth secrets, and maketh known to the king Nebuchadnezzar what shall be in the latter days. Thy dream, and the visions of thy head upon thy bed, are these;

Daniel 2:31-35

31Thou, O king, sawest, and behold a great image. This great image, whose brightness *was* excellent, stood before thee; and the form thereof *was* terrible.

32This image's head *was* of fine gold, his breast and his arms of silver, his belly and his thighs of brass,

33His legs of iron, his feet part of iron and part of clay.

34Thou sawest till that a stone was cut out without hands, which smote the image upon his feet *that were* of iron and clay, and brake them to pieces.

35Then was the iron, the clay, the brass, the silver, and the gold, broken to pieces together, and became like the chaff of the summer threshing floors; and the wind carried them away, that no place was found for them: and the stone that smote the image became a great mountain, and filled the whole earth.

This was the dream the King had and now let's read what God told him and also us in theses latter days the interpretation of the dream.

Daniel 2:36-44

36This *is* the dream; and we will tell the interpretation thereof before the king.

37Thou, O king, *art* a king of kings: for the God of heaven hath given thee a kingdom, power, and strength, and glory.

38And wheresoever the children of men dwell, the beasts of the field and the fowls of the heaven hath he given into thine hand, and hath made thee ruler over them all. Thou *art* this head of gold.

39And after thee shall arise another kingdom inferior to thee, and another third kingdom of brass, which shall bear rule over all the earth.

40And the fourth kingdom shall be strong as iron: forasmuch as iron breaketh in pieces and subdueth all *things*: and as iron that breaketh all these, shall it break in pieces and bruise.

41And whereas thou sawest the feet and toes, part of potters' clay, and part of iron, the kingdom shall be divided; but there shall be in it of the strength of the iron, forasmuch as thou sawest the iron mixed with miry clay.

42And *as* the toes of the feet *were* part of iron, and part of clay, *so* the kingdom shall be partly strong, and partly broken.

43And whereas thou sawest iron mixed with miry clay, they shall mingle themselves with the seed of men: but they shall not cleave one to another, even as iron is not mixed with clay.

44<u>And in the days of these kings shall the God of heaven set up a kingdom, which shall never be destroyed: and the kingdom shall not be left to other people, *but* it shall break in pieces and consume all these kingdoms, and it shall stand for ever.</u>

So, we read the dream and the interpretation, but does history confirm theses Kingdom existed and in this order; let's review history and see if our historical data matches the bible. God said Nebuchadnezzar was the head of gold. And history records this King reigned from 605 BC until 539 BC and the next king to reign was Cyrus the Great; he ruled the Medo-Persia people and conquered Babylon in the year 539 BC and the Medo-Persia kingdom ruled this area or the known world at this time in history from 539 BC to 331 BC. He was also foretold of his victories and ruled by God in the book of Isaiah,

Isaiah 44:28

28That saith of Cyrus, *He is* my shepherd, and shall perform all my pleasure: even saying to Jerusalem, Thou shalt be built; and to the temple, Thy foundation shall be laid.

God foretold Cyrus would be his servant 130 years before it happened.

The conclusion of this then is that the Medo-Persia reign is the silver part of the giant statue in Nebuchadnezzar's dream.

Next, what do we have? The bronze part of the statue, which would be

Greece or Alexander the Great's empire. Alexander reigned from the fall of the Medo-Persia empire in a battle with the Greeks in 331 BC, making Alexander the ruler of the known world at this time. The Greeks ruled until the Romans defeated them. They ruled from 331 BC until 168 BC and are the bronze part of Nebuchadnezzar's dream of a giant statue.

So far all of the historical accounts fit the prophecies of God from the book of Daniel.

Next in the prophecies God gave Daniel is the legs of iron and the feet of iron and clay.

In 168 BC, Rome defeat the rulers of the Greek empire and became the world ruler at this time in history. The Romans ruled from 168 BC until AD 476 as the world leader and government. During this period of time, Rome was constantly being attacked by different tribes from the surrounding area in what we now call Europe. History shows these tribes weren't really trying to destroy Rome but wanted to be a part of this great empire.

But where did these tribes come from? The answer lies in the overall name of all these tribes collectively as a race. What were they called? They were called Caucasians; but the name doesn't fit this race of people very well. As Black skinned people are referred to as Negro, which means 'black' and these white skin people were called Caucasians, but this word doesn't mean 'white' skinned. So, I ask why were these peoples, who settled in an area now known as Europe, called

Caucasians? Could it be because these tribes crossed the Caucasian mountain range to settle in Europe? And if this is the reason, where did these people originally live?

We have a prophecy given of God in the bible which might give us the answer.

Zechariah 7:14

But I scattered them with a whirlwind among all the nations whom they knew not. Thus, the land was desolate after them, that no man passed through nor returned: for they laid the pleasant land desolate.

Jeremiah 30:11

For I am with thee, saith the LORD, to save thee: though I make a full end of all nations whither I have scattered thee, yet will I not make a full end of thee: but I will correct thee in measure, and will not leave thee altogether unpunished.

2 Kings, 17:6

In the ninth year of Hoshea the king of Assyria took Samaria, and carried Israel away into Assyria, and placed them in Halah and in Habor *by* the river of Gozan, and in the cities of the Mede

.

2 Kings 15:29

In the days of Pekah king of Israel came Tiglathpileser king of Assyria, and took Ijon, and Abelbethmaachah, and Janoah, and Kedesh, and Hazor, and Gilead, and Galilee, all the land of Naphtali, and carried them captive to Assyria.

This scattering of Israel took place before Nebuchadnezzar' dream or Judah went into captive in Babylon. If you check world maps, you'll find a mountain range located between Europe and the land known as Assyria call Caucasia Mountains. I believe the tribes of Israel passed through this mountain range to escape the armies of Nebuchadnezzar when Assyria became weak and was conquered by the Babylonians. These peoples who migrated through these mountains into the area called Europe are the so-called 10 lost tribes of Israel. They were called Caucasians because of where they travelled from and were still known by this name until recent time and were listed on the US census as such until modern times.

This brings us back to the meaning of the 10 toes and the miry clay mx of Nebuchadnezzar' dream of a great statue.

In the year 476 AD, Rome was divided. The empire had grown so large, the emperor couldn't govern the whole empire from Rome.

Previously, in Ad 326, Constantine became Emperor by defeating all the small faction within the empire and he said this happened because an angel visited him and told him to use the sign of the cross if he wanted victory. He painted the sign of the cross on all his men's shields and he was victorious. It is said, Rome became a Christen Nation at this time in history. The old 'Sun Worship' of Nimrod and Semiramis became the new Christian Religion of Rome. The 'Madonna and child became Virgin Mary and baby Jesus; the statue of Zeus became Peter the disciple. Saturday, the Sabbath of the Lord was change to Sunday, the worship of the Sun. The people of that day accepted this change because the Jews were accused of killing the Christ, when in reality, the Kenites were the ones responsible for his death on a Roman cross.

Clay, dirt, and etc are the same in the bible usage. We are made of clay or dirt; when we die, the body of all physical being turn back to dirt or clay.

Hence the 10 toes of Nebuchadnezzar' statue being clay and iron gives me this thought or meaning. The ten toes represent ten Nations or 10 tribes mingling with the iron rule of Rome. These tribes are the same ones who crossed the Caucasian Mountains and were a thorn in Rome's side until after 476

A.D. when the Roman Kingdom was divided.

<u>Jeremiah 18:6</u>

O house of Israel, cannot I do with you as this potter? saith the LORD. Behold, as the clay is in the potter's hand, so are ye in mine hand, O house of Israel.

Daniel 7:3-8

(**3**) <u>And four great beasts came up from the sea, diverse one from another.</u>

(**4**) <u>The first *was* like a lion, and had eagle's wings: I beheld till the wings thereof were plucked, and it was lifted up from the earth, and made stand upon the feet as a man, and a man's heart was given to it.</u>

(**5**) And behold another beast, a second, like to a bear, and it raised up itself on one side, and *it had* three ribs in the mouth of it between the teeth of it: and they said thus unto it, Arise, devour much flesh.

(**6**) After this I beheld, and lo another, like a leopard, which had upon the back of it four wings of a fowl; the beast had also four heads; and dominion was given to it.

(**7**) After this I saw in the night visions, and behold a fourth beast, dreadful and terrible, and strong exceedingly; and it had great iron teeth: it devoured and brake in pieces, and stamped the residue with the feet of it: and it *was* diverse from all the beasts that *were* before it; and it had ten horns.

(8) <u>I considered the horns, and, behold, there came up among them another little horn, before whom there were three of the first horns plucked up by the roots: and, behold, in this horn *were* eyes like the eyes of man, and a mouth speaking great things.</u>

Remember in Biblical Symbolism,

Sea = people, lion with wings = Nebuchadnezzar' kingdom.

Bear =strength, Medo-Persia was merciless and destroyed all in its path, = silver arms and chest of Nebuchadnezzar' dream.

The third beast like a leopard with four wings and four heads. The same defines Alexander's Greek kingdom. Alexander's success was credited mostly to his troops being in good physical shape where they could march all night and still fight strong the net day. When Alexander died, his kingdom was divided into four parts, hence the four heads.

The fourth beast exceedingly strong with iron teeth and 10 horns. Same beast we read about earlier; the beast is the Roman Empire, just described a little different. All these beasts are the same as given in Daniel, chapter 2. But here we see a little more information is given about this last beast.

This last beast has 10 horns on its head and a little horn came up among the 10 horns and plucked up three of the horns. Keep in mind, this is the 10 tribes who had made war against Rome and are called Caucasians and are scattered all over the area we know today as Europe. This happened after 476 AD.

Horns = power, or a king, kingdom.

Little horn with eyes of a man and speaking great things; this would have to be a small kingdom and a powerful king.

In 538 AD after Rome was divided, the western half was given to the leader of the Church by Emperor Justinian. Thus, the Papacy became sole dictator of military, spiritual, and commerce of the western half of the Roman Empire. This half of the Empire was ruled by the Papacy from 538 AD until 1798 AD: a total of 1260 years. The power of the Papacy was taken away in 1798 by Napoleon Bonaparte.

Also, noteworthy of thought, when the Vatican was formed, three of the ten tribes fighting against Rome became extinct.

The Ten Tribes are:

Alemanni------------Germany

Burgundians ------------Swiss

Franks ------------------French

Saxons ----------------English

Suevi -------------- Portuguese

Visigoths -------------- Spanish

Herculin ----------------Extinct

Ostrogoths ------------Extinct

Vandals -------------- Extinct

At least 5 attempts have been made to consolidate these tribes and the Roman Empire in the past and all attempt have failed.

Those who tried are:

Charlemagne ---768 AD to 814 AD

Charles V -----1519 AD to 1556 AD

Louis IV ------ 1643 AD to 1715 AD

Napoleon Bonaparte ----- 1804 AD to 1814 AD

Adolf Hitler---1934 AD to 1945 AD

All have failed. Why? It is because God has stated, the final kingdom will be his and He will rule it forever.

Waters ===peoples, multitudes, Nations, and tongues.

Revelation 17:15

15<u>And he saith unto me, the waters which thou sawest, where the whore</u>

sitteth, are peoples, and multitudes, and nations, and tongues.

Revelation 13:1-5

(1) And I stood upon the sand of the sea, and saw a beast rise up out of the sea, having seven heads and ten horns, and upon his horns ten crowns, and upon his heads the name of blasphemy.
(**2**) And the beast which I saw was like unto a leopard, and his feet were as *the feet* of a bear, and his mouth as the mouth of a lion: and the dragon gave him his power, and his seat, and great authority.
(**3**) And I saw one of his heads as it were wounded to death; and his deadly

wound was healed: and all the world wondered after the beast.

(**4**) And they worshipped the dragon which gave power unto the beast: and they worshipped the beast, saying, Who *is* like unto the beast? who is able to make war with him?

(**5**) And there was given unto him a mouth speaking great things and blasphemies; and power was given unto him to continue forty *and* two months.

Don't be shocked, this is the same beasts we read about in Daniel chapters 2 and 7. Only now, the beast has consolidated three of the heads and rules the other seven. They are still separate Nations and have a King or ruling type of government. But spiritually, they are under control of the beast with the seven heads and 10 horns. In other words, the Papacy of the Vatican. The Dragon is the Pope.

As I said earlier the Papacy ruled rom 538 AD until 1798 AD, a total of 1260 years.

42 months @ 30 days to a month =1260 days. One day equals one year, 538 AD to 1798 AD =1260 years.

About the Author

Mr. Hathcock graduated from Almeda University with a master's degree in Religious Theology. He has written several books and commentaries on understanding the Bible, including "Revelation Simplified", "A Path Thru the Weeds". There are a number of "fictional works to his name; namely "Tumbleweed" and "Louisiana Heart"; also "Tree" and "Rockirock". To date, Mr. Hathcock has about 12 or so books listed on the Amazon web site.